Find Your Time:

Assess, Plan, Do, Check, Review

Sandie Barrie

Barrie Enterprises

barrieenterprises@charter.net

Copyright © 2009 Barrie Enterprises, Sparks, NV

This edition produced by CreateSpace in association with Barrie Enterprises. (www.findyourtime.org).

Assistant Copy Editor: Megan Moyer

ISBN – 13   978-0-9840953-0-8

ISBN – 10   0-9840953-0-6

All rights reserved, including the right to reproduce this book or portions thereof in any form whatsoever. For requests to print, contact the publisher at barrieenterprises@charter.net.

This publication contains the opinions and ideas of its author. The material provides helpful information on time management. Neither the author nor the publisher are engaged in rendering medical, health, financial, or any other kind of personal services through the sale of this book.

The author and publisher specifically disclaim all responsibility for any liability, loss or risk, personal or otherwise, which is incurred as a consequence, directly or indirectly; from the use and application of any of the contents in this book.

There are several websites, which provide additional references for the reader. Websites are not static and may change with time. You can let the publisher know when a link is not working by sending an email to barrieenterprises@charter.net.

Dedication

To all the people who taught me valuable lessons about using change theory and the quality improvement model; and
to those who will gain a greater degree of happiness when they discover the quality improvement model's simplicity and energy in finding their time.

Hopefully, Emily, AJ, Alayna, Alison, and Kamryn will learn about change theory and the quality improvement model early in life and will teach it to their children.

Table of Contents

SECTION 1 - INTRODUCTION 1
    What this Book is Not About 3
    About the Book 3
    About the Author 4

SECTION 2 - CHANGE THEORY 7

SECTION 3 – QUALITY IMPROVEMENT MODEL 11
    Components 12
    Putting the Components Together 16

SECTION 4 – TIME MANAGEMENT TOOLS 21
    Technological Tools 21
    Non-technological Tools 27

SECTION 5 – USING TIME TO MANAGE LIFE DIMENSIONS 31

Health 33
    Improving Your Weight 34
    Managing Chronic Pain 38
    Establishing a Home Medical Record 41

Food 46
    Making Good Choices About Where to Eat 46
    Doing Meal Preparation and Clean-Up 51
    Organizing for Purchasing Groceries and Household Items 55

Household Maintenance 60
    Recycling Daily 60
    Reducing Time Spent Doing Laundry 63
    Taking Pictures of Possessions 67

Travel 72
    Planning Trips 72
    Maintaining Vehicles 75
    Reducing Travel Annoyances 79

Finances 83
    Reducing Fear in Developing an Operating Budget 84
    Saving Money 87
    Taking Control of Investments... 91

Work 95
    Ongoing Preparation for Changing Your Career 95
    Employing Volunteerism in Finding New Work 100
    Readying the Resume 103

Education 107
    Making Good Choices in Deciding on College/Technical Work 108
    Going to Class 113
    Completing Requirements/Assignments for Classes 117

Hobbies 122
    Learning How to Sew 122
    Choosing Between Options When Looking at Hobbies..................................... 126
    Discovering Persistence When You Decide To Write 130

Service Opportunities 137
    Writing Proposals for Short-term Projects 137
    Maximizing Energy in Long-term Projects 142
    Building on Using Groups of People in Lifelong Projects 147

Building Relationships 153
    Creating Contacts for the Family 153
    Preparing Agendas When Dealing with Professionals 156
    Cherishing Options When Making Friends 160

SECTION 6 – BLENDING YOUR CHANGE WITH THE CHANGE OF OTHERS. 165
    Daily and Weekly Review 166
    Learn Tools 166
    Nurture Relationships 166
    Perception is Everything 167
    Keep Priorities Straight 167
    Maintain Open Options 168
    Understand Your Values 168
    Balance Persistence and Patience 168
    Be Considerate 169
    Setting Your Own Pace 169
    Keep in the Present 170
    Smile 170

SECTION 7 – TIME MANAGEMENT TEMPLATE 171

SECTION 8 – LAST THOUGHTS 175

APPENDIX A – PERFORMANCE INDICATORS DASHBOARD BY MONTH 179

APPENDIX B – EXAMPLES: QUALITY IMPROVEMENT OPPORTUNITIES 183

APPENDIX C – WRITING A PROPOSAL USING SOPPADA FORMAT 185

SELECTED RESOURCES 187

ENDNOTES 197

BIBLIOGRAPHY 201

AUTHOR INDEX 203

Section 1 - Introduction

I have been watching Oprah for more years than I can remember. Oprah probably does not realize that her television programs reflect components of the quality improvement model. Just think about how Oprah tries to get her viewers to **assess** how they can do something differently; or **plan** to take their lunch while they stand in line to vote; or **do** something like exercise; or cautions her viewers to **check** on their finances; or how she warns to **review** our personal safety. However, Oprah does not use the quality improvement model in its entirety for any one show. Recently, I have been having great fun watching her shows and putting the show content into the different components of the quality improvement model. Oprah could use the quality improvement model in the design of her shows to demonstrate a systematic method to examine any of the issues that she explores.

The purpose of this first edition of *Find Your Time: Assess, Plan, Do, Check, Review* is to demonstrate how to use change theory and the quality improvement model to improve one's life by finding and managing your time. Many business books provide tips on how to save time. The difference with this book is that the focus is on putting a system in place to save time in one's personal life based on life dimensions. The reader learns how to focus their time by eliminating waste and making better use of their time. Any one life has many dimensions. A dimension is an aspect that a person has to deal with on a daily basis. The book focuses on the following 10 life dimensions: health, food, household maintenance, travel, finances, work, education, hobbies, service opportunities, and building relationships. The information is pertinent to individuals of varying generations and ethnic diversities.

The word "find" means, "to come upon by searching or effort"[1]. The intention is to demonstrate to readers how they can find and manage their time by using the quality improvement model. The quality improvement model provides a systematic framework to make positive changes in one's life through better management of time.

Section 2 supplies insights into basic change theory by examining the stages an individual goes through when involved in change. Section 3 describes the components of the quality improvement model: assess, plan, do, check, and review. The major purpose for the quality improvement model is to demonstrate a systematic method to accomplish change. The reader learns how to eliminate waste or make better use of their time by setting up a system of time management that emphasizes choosing between options and evaluating progress over time.

Section 4 identifies tools that will help the reader use the quality improvement model in the technological age. The reader can also use non-technological tools, since clocks and paper continue to be useful tools in managing time.

Section 5 contains examples for using the quality improvement model to manage ones time. A friendly, light voice presents the material for 30 every-day situations. Lessons learned by the author are shared demonstrating how when one option does not work, the user needs to seek out additional approaches until success is reached. Persistence is a friend in using the quality improvement model.

Section 6 provides a discussion on how you need to blend the time management strategies you desire with the time management strategies desired by your family, friends, and co-workers. Section 7 supplies a time management template using the quality improvement model for the reader to use to start on their own journey to find and manage their time.

To finish, Section 8 provides my last thoughts on how change theory and the quality improvement model have helped me in developing and increasing happiness in my life.

There are three appendices. The first offers examples of performance indicators as they relate to 30 everyday situations, such as purchasing groceries, from the 10 life dimensions presented. The second appendix suggests other examples of situations where applying the quality improvement model can help you find your time. The third appendix provides a guide for writing proposals. Suggestions for reference materials are found in the Selected Resources Section, providing the reader more in-depth information about topics discussed in *Find Your Time: Assess, Plan, Do, Check, Review*.

What this Book is Not About

You know the type of person who asks questions all the time, expecting you to get the answers. It could be your boss, your spouse, or a close friend. This takes up an enormous amount of your time and takes away from what interests you have and what you want to think about and look into. At times, you may want to liberate yourself from your boss's interruptions. However, you may not want to change your spouse or the close friend and the interruptions they bring into your life. *Find Your Time: Assess, Plan, Do, Check, Review* will not teach you how to manage interruptions or misuse of your time (see Selected Resources).

Are you always doing something for others that they could do, and in some cases really should do, for themselves? Frequently these tasks are not what interests you or what you want to spend your time on doing. *Find Your Time: Assess, Plan, Do, Check, Review* will <u>not</u> help you stop *others* from managing your time. You will have to look to other resources for help in sorting out these requests (see Selected Resources).

Do you live with someone who is always putting something off, who just can't quite get to finish the last had-to-do-it project? *Find Your Time: Assess, Plan, Do, Check, Review* is <u>not</u> about dealing with procrastination, which is a huge time waster (see Selected Resources).

How many books have you read that have tips on how to save time? A list of items might provide some stimulation for managing your time, but it does not place the actions within a systematic framework to sustain the change. *Find Your Time: Assess, Plan, Do, Check, Act* is <u>not</u> about providing tips to save time (see Selected Resources).

About the Book

Time has an element of past, present, and future. *Find Your Time: Assess, Plan, Do, Check, Review* focuses on the present and future elements of time, but uses the past element to assist the reader in making the model operational. The book was developed using Microsoft Word 2003. Barrie Enterprises sent the book file via the Internet to the CreateSpace portal on Amazon.com, which is a self-publishing company. CreateSpace at http://www.createspace.com used the portable document file (pdf) to print and bind the book and made it available for purchase. This method of developing the perfect bound book avoids any waste or expense from over-publishing. Book production occurs only when a book is ordered. You can purchase a downloadable copy and if you have access to the Internet, the reference links are live, making it easy to find the materials referenced without retyping the address into the browser. *Find Your Time: Assess, Plan, Do, Check, Review* not only helps you determine if you are ready for change and provides a useful quality improvement model to help manage your change, it also serves to demonstrate that anyone can write a book and self-publish it quickly at a very low cost. See http://www.findyourtime.org for more details.

On Oprah's show, she indicates she uses a Post-it Highlighter Pen with 50 Flags as she reads a book. You can find one at http://www.Amazon.com – or almost any office supply store. You may find something like this helpful as you read the pages of this book and find areas that you want to mark up for further review and investigation.

About the Author

Sandie Barrie has a Ph.D. in Applied Management and Decision Sciences from Walden University in Minneapolis, MN. She has been married to the same practical man for 42 years, has three children and five grandchildren. Barrie is a registered nurse and she has focused 20 years of her nursing career around bedside nursing. She has worked in facilities for the mentally ill and mentally retarded; nursing homes; and small and large hospitals. For 10 years, Barrie devoted her time to hospital performance (quality) improvement and case management programs. For five years, she worked on a variety of healthcare projects that included collecting data on nursing home patients, completing utilization review functions, and working on state and national health care initiatives regarding patient safety and hospital/nursing home performance improvement indicators. During the last five years, Barrie worked with an employer coalition where she facilitated education to employers on health care initiatives in a series called, "Building Common Knowledge" along with being the Nevada Coordinator for the Leapfrog Hospital Patient Safety Initiative. Barrie has established her public writing career with her first book, *Find Your Time: Assess, Plan, Do, Check, Review.*

If you have comments for the author, send to findyourtime@charter.net. Enjoy!

Section 2 - Change Theory

Don't let the word "theory" scare you. The word theory simply means "the analysis of a set of facts in their relation to one another"[2]. Another word, "change" means "to make a shift from one to another"[3]. Put the two words together and the following concept for "change theory" emerges, which is the "expectation that we can make a shift from one way to another based on an analysis of a set of facts." In order to get something different in your life, you need to manage your time differently. Let's start our discussion by looking first at change theory and then we will proceed to Section 3 to look at quality improvement models.

There are many books on change and its implications for organizations. Marketers study change theory so they can predict how a product will sell. Change theory provides individuals with a process to determine if they are ready to go about doing something different for the problems they are solving and the decisions they are making. Several iterations for change theory exist where some stages in the process are included in certain models, but are not present in other models. Let's look at two prominent thinkers on this topic, Everett Rogers and James Prochaska. These two writers have dedicated their entire careers to studying the topic of change and providing somewhat similar models to describe change theory.

The first well-respected writer, Rogers, developed five stages in the Innovation-Decision Process that include:

- Knowledge stage – where the individual learns of new change and gains some understanding of how it works;
- Persuasion stage – where the individual forms an opinion about the new change; whether it be favorable or unfavorable;
- Decision stage – where the individual engages in activities that lead to choosing whether to accept or reject the new change;
- Implementation stage – occurs when the individual puts the new change into use; and

- Confirmation stage – when the individual seeks reinforcement about the new change and can even reverse a previous decision.[4]

Besides looking at the stages that an individual moves through, additional research completed by Rogers looks at the rate that individuals make changes. In the *Diffusion of Innovations*, Rogers classifies individuals into five major categories as they adapt to change. These labels for an individual include:

- Innovators – venturesome, desires new ideas and brings them into the system boundary from the outside;
- Early Adopters – respectful, has opinion leadership and provides advice and information about new ideas;
- Early Majority – deliberate, interacting with peers and adopts new ideas just before the average member in a system;
- Late Majority – skeptical, adopting new ideas just after the average member in a system; and
- Laggards – traditional, last one to adopt new ideas.[5]

According to a second respected writer, Prochaska et al., change theory has six stages that an individual moves through in making a change. These six stages include:

- Pre-contemplation – no intent to change in near future;
- Contemplation – openly states intention to change within the next six months;
- Preparation – intends to make steps for a change, usually within the next month;
- Action – overt activity occurs but generally has not been sustained for six months;
- Maintenance – effective change occurs with few to no relapses; and
- Termination – action no longer necessary, change has occurred.[6]

What is Coming Up?

Section 2 has glazed over major works completed on change theory. See Selected Resources for additional information. Next, in Section 3, the quality improvement model is described and links between the major writers on change theory and quality improvement models are briefly discussed.

Section 3 – Quality Improvement Model

Wikipedia is a new way to look up the meaning of terms on the Internet. Wikipedia is "written collaboratively by volunteers from all around the world"[7]. Using Wikipedia, the term "quality improvement" means "purposeful change to a process to obtain a reliable outcome."[8] and "model" is a "pattern or description that shows how something can work or function."[9] Thus, a quality improvement model demonstrates how to apply a pattern of activities (model) to change a process to obtain a reliable outcome. William Edwards Deming[10] is the father of the quality improvement movement. Walter Shewhart[11] in 1924 developed the control chart, which served to support the work completed by Deming. Simply, a control chart is used to predict whether the process being monitored is in control or not and underpins the quality improvement model. The quality improvement model that most recognize has "plan, do, check, act" as its mantra.

The quality improvement model used here is an adaptation of the works completed by Shewhart[12] and Deming[13] and holds tenets from the works of Rogers[14] and Prochaska[15]. As you grow in the development of your understanding of change theory and quality improvement models you will be able to understand why and how change occurs and how you can make change work for you to obtain goals and objectives you desire.

The core of the quality improvement model is time management. The structural frame or components for the model consist of five words: assess, plan, do, check, and review. The Barrie Quality Improvement Model™ is referred to as the quality improvement model. Visualize the components as a circular process or steps taken in order to accomplish the outcome desired. Below is a brief description of the five components of the quality improvement model. Figure 1 below provides a way to cement the components of the model into our minds.

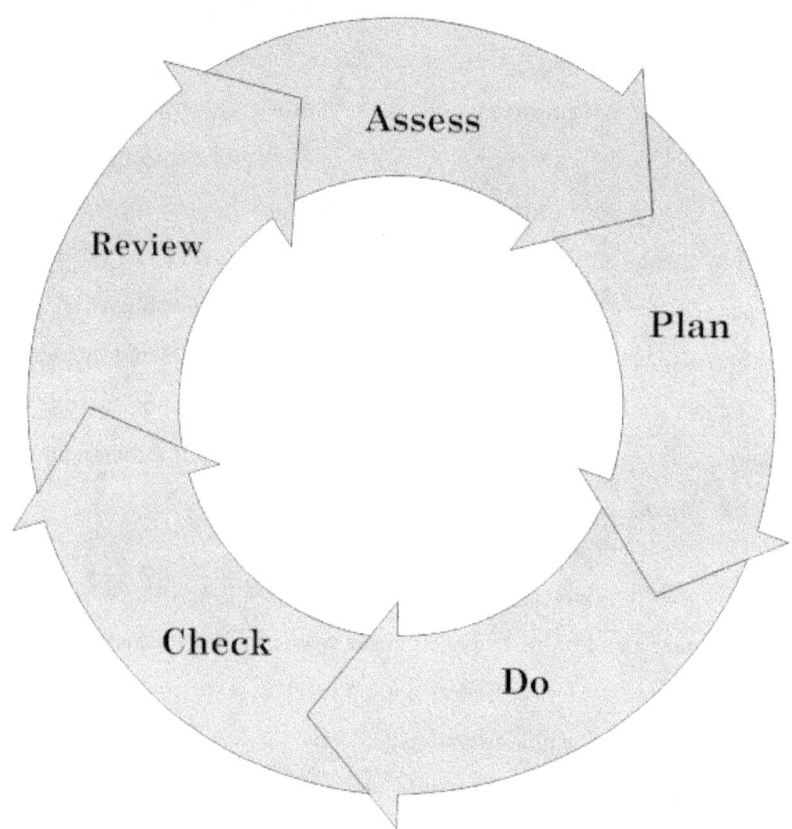

Figure 1. Barrie Quality Improvement Model ™

Components

The quality improvement model has five steps: assess, plan, do, check and review. A short explanation of each component follows.

Assess

The step of assessing added to Shewhart and Deming's initial work provides a place to start the model. It is time to begin and you are not sure how to do an assessment. Assessment is simply asking questions that start with the following words: how, when, where, what, and why. What improvements are possible? An important point is to make sure that you are asking the right questions.

Plan

A plan is a short statement of what actions need to be taken to solve the problem and is based on several factors that include: looking at the current research, looking at what has worked for others, and looking at what is doable with the amount of time that is available to solve the problem or make an improvement. When I am starting to write a plan, I often go to the Internet and Google (the new verb for searching something through a popular website called Google) the term and review what is online. I go to http://www.amazon.com and search for books on the topic. I ask my friends and colleagues what they know or have learned about the topic since there is nothing like topic experience. I get a sense in my mind of how long I have to work on the plan to obtain the change desired.

In fact, frequently when I am working with others on their use of the quality improvement model, I will ask the question, "How much time do you have to work on this problem/topic/opportunity for improvement?" I have learned having a sense of the time period helps in selecting the goals, objectives, and performance indicators for the problem/topic/opportunity for improvement, thus helping the process get started. For no matter what you do when you use the quality improvement model, it must be realistic and usable.

Learning how to write goals and objectives is beyond the scope of this book (see Selected Resources). The goal one desires reflects in a broad statement, a goal. Objectives are precise and concrete statements that set opportunities for improvement. Objectives reflect the intended future. Performance indicators demonstrate what is occurring now. As part of the plan, outcome indicators to measure performance are critical for success in using the quality improvement model and need to be set prior to taking action within a specific time period. A performance indicator is a measurable signal, which reflects the current condition or outcome desired.

The plan consists at a minimum, of a goal (long-range), objectives (future condition), and performance indicators (current condition). Writing the plan down will help you remember what you decided to do. Again, the quality improvement model will not help you if you think writing a plan is for someone else – it's for you! Remember, a plan can start with a small trial, or by taking a sample, or by doing a pilot before one decides to go into the full plan.

Do

The word "do" implies action. After assessing the problem or opportunity for improvement and developing a plan, you must then take action. There are many reasons why you may not take action at this time. You may become ill during the process, the problem rectifies itself without action, or you may learn something during the process of planning that changes your perception on the significance of what the problem is or what the opportunity for improvement should be. Working off a written plan with specific objectives should increase your desire to take action. There are many excuses for not following through with the plan, but for the quality improvement model to work, action is essential. In fact, a constant question is, "What is the next step or action to be taken?" A check sheet easily facilitates keeping track of your actions over time.

Periodically, you should study the check sheet to make sure you are completing it correctly and consistently. More than once I have designed a check sheet and found that in practice, it was not measuring what needed measurement. Using your calendar to remind you to complete the check sheet is helpful in getting you into the new habit. Making the check sheet readily available is important. Try putting the check sheet on your bathroom mirror or the refrigerator to help you remember. Placing review dates in Microsoft Outlook 2003 helps to ensure review of the performance indicator(s) occurs. Taking a few measurements is important for the use of the quality improvement model. It is easy to do – simply identify how you will know if you have been successful in solving your problem or in evaluating the opportunity for improvement. How can you measure the improvement in numbers? For instance, if you take your weight on the last day of each month, you can determine if you are gaining or losing weight. If you look at your bank balance at the end of each month, you can determine if you are saving more money or not.

Check

To check simply means to do some analysis! It may seem like extra work to use indicators to measure the current progress. However, executing a plan and then taking measurement helps you see whether your plan and its associated strategies and tactics are working.

Compare the measurement of performance indicators to looking at the dashboard of a car: you can check the amount of gas, whether the car is getting too hot, how fast you're going, or how many miles you have driven. Appendix A provides a table demonstrating a performance indicators dashboard for some of the 30 situations examined in Section 5. Reviewing performance indicators periodically (generally by month) will help you monitor the dimensions of your life and the situations you desire to change.

Review

In adapting the common model from "plan, do, check, act" established by Shewhart and Deming to "assess, plan, do, check, review" intentionally puts emphasis on the last component, which is the review component. The review component brings closure or termination to the model if the change has occurred. Taking the time to review the plan, the data collected on the check sheets for the performance indicators, and doing some simple analysis demonstrates satisfaction that the plan has worked, or is working, or it lets you know you need to alter the original plan to be able to accomplish the change you desire. The strength of the quality improvement model comes with not giving up too soon and learning that if one option has not worked, you need to determine what needs to happen to make it work and start the quality improvement model over again. Setting up a simple table allows you to look at all the indicators that you want to monitor for all the life dimensions (see Appendix A).

Another element of the review component is realizing that if the plan and actions have been successful, the user needs to share the accomplishment to assist others and to embed the change into society's culture. For instance, surgeons will tell you they saw one (surgery), then they did one (surgery), and then they taught one (surgery). Using the quality improvement model is how you learn to correct your mistakes, use options when needed to make improvements, and then teach others so they do not have to make the same mistakes. Lessons learned are invaluable to society. We need to share them shamelessly.

When an individual is ready to make a change, using a quality improvement model can be very useful in the process to be able to obtain sustained change. It should be noted that individuals who have moved into the decision stage of Rogers' change model or the action stage in Prochaska's change model will have the most success. If an individual tries to use the quality improvement model too early in their change process, he may become frustrated because he may lack the desire, motivation, and work ethic required to make change.

Putting the Components Together

Let's look at one example to get us started at learning how to use the quality improvement model. A simple example demonstrates the whole process. Let's look at weight. Say you just came from the doctor's office after your annual physical and she told you that you are overweight and you should lose some weight. Assuming that you agree with your doctor and have been contemplating her comments and have decided that yes, you are ready to lose weight, you can use the quality improvement model to help you along the way. First, let's look at assessing weight.

Assess
- How tall are you?
- How much do you weigh?

Plan
After you have completed the assessment, you can do some research to see what an ideal weight for your size should be. Using the Internet, go to the following website: http://www.nhlbisupport.com/bmi/bmicalc.htm and enter your weight and height. Let's use my data as an example. I put in 5 feet, 0 inches and 137 pounds. Selecting the "Compute

BMI" button, I find my Body Mass Index or BMI shows that I am overweight at 26.8. While the following is extremely simplified, further research demonstrates that to lose weight, I need to cut my calories and move around more. A plan is not complex, is generally one page in length, and may only take a few lines.

Goal - long-range:

- Lose weight to improve personal health

Objective(s) – future condition(s):

- Decrease current weight of 137 pounds by 1 pound in 4 weeks by cutting down my portions of food and walking around the block 4 days each week.

Performance Indicator(s) - current condition:

- Current weight monthly
- Current BMI monthly

Do

Developing a simple check sheet to measure the daily portion intake and weekly exercise is important to capture data in real time. In order to ensure that I see my plan everyday, I tape the check sheet (see Table 1 below) to my bathroom mirror and put a pencil close by so that I can check off whether I have accomplished my task each day.

Table 1 - Check Sheet for Daily Portion Intake and Weekly Exercise

Month – February	Starting Weight – 137 pounds	
Day of Week	Ate Small Portions	Walked Around Block
Sunday		
Monday	√	
Tuesday	√	√
Wednesday	√	√
Thursday		√
Friday	√	√

Sandie Barrie

Month – February	Starting Weight – 137 pounds	
Day of Week	Ate Small Portions	Walked Around Block
Saturday		
Sunday		
Monday	√	
Tuesday		
Wednesday	√	√
Thursday	√	√
Friday	√	
Saturday		
Sunday		
Monday	√	√
Tuesday	√	
Wednesday		
Thursday		√
Friday	√	√
Saturday		√
Sunday		√
Monday	√	
Tuesday	√	√
Wednesday	√	
Thursday	√	√
Friday	√	√
Saturday		
Ending Weight	136 pounds	

For the next 28 days, when I am in the bathroom, I will have to face the mirror and tick off whether I have eaten smaller portions or walked around the block. The hardest part may be not tearing the piece of paper off the mirror. At the end of the month when I am going to weigh again, I use the same scale at the same time of day and see what the results are.

Check

It is time for analysis. I take the information from the check sheet and see that I have lost one pound. I analyze my check sheet and see that on 16 days, I ate smaller portions, and for three out of four weeks, I walked around the block on four days.

Review

I congratulate myself on the one-pound loss in weight. But for the quality improvement model to work in its entirety, I need to take the final step of acting on reviewing my initial goals and objectives, reviewing the check sheet and looking at the performance indicators that I have chosen to monitor monthly, weight and BMI. Here is my analysis. In order to get to a ideal weight, as reflected by the BMI, I need to get to 127 pounds, which means I need to lose 10 more pounds. Now, I have some information that I can use to make my next goal, which is to lose the additional 10 pounds to get to an acceptable BMI of 24.8. I can determine if I want to take six months to accomplish this goal or I can change my plan, to increase my exercise to lose the weight a little faster but at a safe rate – say, two pounds per month. The second option will require me to change my initial plan or increase my compliance with my current plan. Section 5 provides an in-depth discussion on weight.

Once I am at the desired weight, I can continue to monitor my weight and BMI monthly to ensure that I do not slowly put weight back on and I can add these two indicators to my performance indicators dashboard (see Appendix A) that shows what is reviewed monthly. In the review process, the realization of the quality improvement model occurs with improved outcomes.

What is Coming Up?

Section 3 has described the quality improvement model: assess, plan, do, check, review. A simple example demonstrated how the quality improvement model when used to improve overall personal health results in weight reduction. Section 5 provides more on weight loss.

Sandie Barrie

Section 4 describes available technological and non-technological tools that can help you learn to incorporate the quality improvement model into your daily lives to manage your time.

Section 4 – Time Management Tools

Now that you understand how the components of the quality improvement model work together, you need some tools to assist you in its use. When you think of the word "tool," you have many mental representations depending on how you have used tools in your life. It could be a shovel to move dirt, a hammer to nail a wall together, or a sewing machine to put two pieces of cloth together. As you explore ways to find your time, you have many tools that can help you in the process of putting the model to work. At first, it may not be easy to see the Internet and its associated applications as tools, but they serve as important methods of assistance to you in using the quality improvement model.

Technological Tools

David Allen describes in his book, *Getting Things Done: The Art of Stress-Free Productivity*[16], what we all know – that we are allowing a mega amount of communication from the outside world into our internal environment that is then generating volumes of ideas for us to deal with in our inner world. All of these communications contribute to new stress as you try to deal with your own needs for change and the need for change that your families, friends and co-workers desire.

In our changing world, you have many new tools that you can use to assist you in managing your time. There are costs to these tools – some of which are in dollars and cents, and some of which are in hours and minutes. Using a hammer to nail a wall together or even to use a sewing machine to sew two pieces of cloth together are rather easy and only take a few minutes to learn. Learning how to make use of the new technological tools that have occurred over the last 20 years can be difficult for some, and they take time to learn to use effectively. Below are a few of the technologies that are available to us. It is beyond the scope of this book to explain how to use these tools (see Selected Resources).

There are costs to all the technological tools. However, one does not have to purchase them and learn them all at the same time. There may be a lot of value gained by adding them one at a time to assist you in managing your life. If you have limited financial resources and/or time to only figure out one of these technologies, the first one to learn is the Internet.

Internet

It is beyond the scope of *Find Your Time: Assess, Plan, Do, Check, Review* to teach its readers how to use the Internet (see Selected Resources). A few suggestions provide some help to get started. Simply, the Internet works by going to a specific web address (which is a series of letters and, occasionally, numbers) and finding information about a myriad of topics that are relevant to our daily lives. The combination of letters and/or numbers forms an address. Search engines, such as Google, utilize addresses to find pertinent information to the search topic. When I was in the third grade learning how to spell, I never envisioned it would be important – essential, really – in my ability to search the World Wide Web.

One learns early that the search engine needs preciseness. If a letter is off, if there is an extra dot in the address, or if a word is misspelled, it simply will not work. A tip is to put your finger over the string of letters or numbers and move your finger along each character as you type. Also double-checking before hitting "enter" will help ensure that the search is successful the first time.

The browsers like Internet Explorer search the World Wide Web. One can store a web site address in a "favorites" section. One of the things I have learned in using the "favorites" section is to make a folder and place similar topics in the same folder. For instance, I have a personal interest in sewing and have fun searching the websites that are relevant to this topic. However, it makes looking these websites up at a later time easier if I place them into a folder labeled "sewing" rather than just saving as a general "favorite." The sewing website is easier to find when one wants to return to it later. Most modern day libraries have access to the Internet making it available to everyone. Even more exciting is realizing that you can save your personal "favorites" list to the World Wide Web, thus being able to access it using any computer connected to the Internet. Check out http://www.diigo.com/index. With diigo, you are able to highlight important elements of the Internet page you are reading and then either save it or send it off to someone. I wish I had had this convenience when I was doing my doctoral studies.

I mentioned Wikipedia earlier. It is an online encyclopedia (edited and updated by the public), which is very useful when you do not know what a word means or you want to get some basic information about a subject. Look at http://www.wikipedia.org/. It is a wealth of knowledge that helps us understand concepts that we encounter and need to be able to understand. Another place to look up a word is at http://www.m-w.com, which is the Merriam-Webster website.

BlackBerry

Maybe you are a homemaker, managing a couple of youngsters; you have a computer and you have heard about a BlackBerry. It may be a little hard to justify this in your budget, but the next time someone wants to buy you a gift, ask them to put the money toward a BlackBerry. A BlackBerry is more than a phone – it also houses a calendar, a "to do" list, a contact list. It allows you to access your e-mail, where you can receive and send e-mail messages and text messages. One can synchronize the applications on the Blackberry with their main computer (see Selected Resources).

Microsoft Products
<u>Outlook</u>

Microsoft Outlook 2003 keeps track of phone numbers, addresses, e-mails, and your calendar. If you have to look up a phone number, address, or other piece of data in the regular telephone book, be sure to enter the information into "contacts" component right away to avoid doing this again. For me, this is annoying because I do not want to stop what I am doing to add the information at that time. However, doing it means I get a little reward the next time I need that information because I do not have to look it up in the phone book again. The contact information can be synched with the BlackBerry so making a change in either calendar the Microsoft Calendar or the BlackBerry makes the change in the other (see Selected Resources).

Sandie Barrie

<u>Microsoft Word 2003</u>

Microsoft Word 2003 provides the writer a method to write a variety of documents, from writing resumes and letters to preparing fliers for the Neighborhood Watch Group you are starting.

<u>Microsoft Excel 2003 and Microsoft Access 2003</u>

Microsoft Excel 2003 and Microsoft Access 2003 are tools used to enter data to keep track of information in databases and spreadsheets. Now, many of us think we can keep everything in our heads, including all the information to manage the maintenance of our vehicles, the appointments we have had with our physicians, and keeping track of all our passwords. In reality, most of us cannot keep track of all this information without some sort of aid. I find Microsoft Excel 2003 and Microsoft Access 2003 to be perfect for these types of jobs. Many people will simply not want to find and invest the time to learn the basics of these programs. However, you will save yourself time and money in the long run You will be able to develop your own spreadsheets and databases and will not be tempted to purchase software packages developed to do self-help specialized tasks, such as developing budgets or inventories of belongings or programs to track passwords.

Online Shopping

Online shopping is popular and is a great way to save time especially in regions of the country where the winters are long and it is difficult to get around. It saves a lot of time finding a specialty item not easily found in local stores. When I can't find something that I need, I simply do a Google search and generally find what I need, purchase online, and save time in the process.

Social Media

During the last year, an explosion has occurred on the Internet with the development and adoption of social media. There are many new opportunities including sites like MySpace, Facebook, LinkedIn, and Twitter. Blogs (personal Web logs dealing with any aspect or interest of a person's life – daily, weekly, etc.) alone provide incredible amount of information by people who are interested in a specific topic. Personally, I have decided that Facebook http://www.facebook.com/SandieBarrie, LinkedIn http://www.linkedin.com/in/sandiebarrie, and Twitter http://twitter.com/SandieBarrie will provide enough of an Internet presence for me. The new social media offers many ways for someone to save time by using each medium in creative ways to make connections with family, friends, and colleagues. There are many books on this topic and you can see my favorite in the Selected Resources section.

Facebook

You may have heard of Facebook – it is an opportunity on the Internet where you can develop a profile of yourself and then develop a group page where you can invite family and friends to join you. By posting information onto the page, you can share information with those you let join the group, like statements about what you are doing, or pictures you took on a trip or a video of a sporting event where your grandson played in the regional playoffs. It has been a great way to meet up with many of my family members, especially those that do not live close to me. In addition, the great thing is – it's free!

LinkedIn

Another popular website is LinkedIn, where again you can create a profile for others to view. The difference is that these are professional profiles, and this site has become a great place to search if you are going to meet with a new attorney, surgeon, or real estate agent to find out something about the individual before you meet with them. It is also a great place to find out about a potential speaker for the next guild meeting. LinkedIn provides a place to examine the credentials of the person you are meeting with when you get the next job interview.

Twitter

Once again, you have to set Twitter up to work with contacts. Using 140 characters and a phone (with Internet capabilities – i.e. the aforementioned BlackBerry), you can communicate within seconds with your family, friends or colleagues and let them know what you are doing now.

MapQuest and Global Positioning Systems

Getting to somewhere you have not been before is a constant struggle. Whether you are walking, driving, or going by bus, having directions to where you are going will help you get there in less time. Using the Internet, you can find out exactly how to get from one place to another by going to http://www.mapquest.com/. It is simple, free, and you can print directions right from the website.

The development of global positioning systems, or GPS, complements MapQuest and provides an electronic method for directions to be verbally given to you as you travel, telling you when and which way you need to turn in order to get to your destination. A fun tool is Google Earth (http://earth.google.com/). Google Earth is also a free tool that allows one to see a three-dimensional picture of where you are going, like looking down from a helicopter. Therefore, when traveling by car, you can print out the MapQuest directions, review where you are going on Google Earth, and then use the GPS to have verbal directions given to you as you drive. Wow… and how did those who came before us get anywhere?

Skype

Wish you could talk to your friends or family more often and actually see a picture of them while you are talking to them? For a free solution, Skype is your answer. All you need to get started is a computer with an Internet connection, a camera, and some downloadable software from http://www.skype.com/. After you sign up and get your family or friends to sign up, you are able to talk with them over the Internet and see their picture on your computer. If you watch Oprah, you would see that she frequently has a guest beamed into her television studio from somewhere around the world using Skype.

Skype has all kinds of applications, from use in day-to-day business needs to talking with people who are across town, across the country, or even across the world. A Skype connection is a great way to keep in touch with an elderly person by simply going to their home or nursing home and setting up the process and writing a few directions down so they can turn on the equipment. There is nothing like a picture to let you know that while mom or dad sound good on the phone they look good as well. College students studying in another state or country can see family members and enjoy the new birth, the high school graduation party, or just a couple of words with someone they love.

Craigslist

Do you need to buy or sell something, look for a job, find a place to rent, or wonder if someone may be going to a basketball game in another town and looking for a ride? Craigslist can be your answer.

If you want to find a Craigslist listing close by, just go to http://www.craigslist.org and browse for activity for city near you. Once you get into the website, you can establish an account (although it's not necessary), and then you can post to a variety of topics (see Table 2 below). You post to a single geographic area and category at a time and the posting expires from the site in 30 days. See Table 2 for a list of topics on Craigslist.

Table 2 – Topics Available on Craigslist

Community	Job Offered	Resume/Job Wanted
Event	Housing Offered	Housing Wanted
Personal/Romance	For Sale	Item Wanted
Discussion Forums	Gig Offered	Service Offered

Non-technological Tools

Not everyone can make use of the technological tools for a variety of reasons. The Internet and its associated hardware and software tools are relatively new. Before they were in existence, a basic clock and paper were the main tools used to assist in managing time. Clocks and paper are still valuable tools to manage time. Use these alone or with the technological tools described above.

Sandie Barrie

Call-up File

Are you always losing valuable paperwork? Starting a call-up file will save you hours of time annually since you will be able to find needed paperwork much easier. To make a call-up file, simply take 31 file folders and label them from 1 to 31, one folder for each day of the month. Then you have a place to put important pieces of paper on the day that you need them. You also keep extra paper off the top of your kitchen table or desk avoiding paper mix-ups. I have tried to use monthly files, but find that my life does not reach that far out and that the 31-day call-up file is the most useful.

As I begin a new project, such as starting a small business and writing this book, I start a specific call-up file for each project. I have used call-up files for more than 20 years in my professional and personal life. For the last 10 years, I have not had the luxury of a personal assistant. Frankly, at first I thought I could not live without someone helping me manage my paper and my responsibilities. Now, I am not sure that I would want to go back to having a personal assistant because I have trained myself to handle my papers and put them where I want them so I can find them when I need them.

Allen reinforces something that I have used for years in my work and what he calls the critical success factor, which is the use of the "weekly review."[17] Allen notes that our mind needs help in remembering and reminding you about those actions that you have planned to take. Therefore, once a week I go through the call-up file. I have found weekly reviews useful to make sure that I don't forget about something that I want to do, especially if it has to do with paper. The key here is placing the weekly review task right into your calendar as an appointment and then taking the time to review what is in the call-up file.

I use Julie Morgenstern's system of deleting, delaying, diminishing, or delegating to handle the paper during the weekly review.[18] I can throw the file out or move it to the reference file system. I can change the day I intend to take action on the item, making sure that I change my calendar reminders. I can determine if I really need the project and if it is important enough to remain in my call-up file or I can discard it. I can pull the file out and delegate it to someone else if I have that option and it is appropriate. When I file paper, I place the most current piece of paper on top of the other papers in the file.

What is Coming Up?

Section 4 has described technological and non-technological tools. These tools will help users of the quality improvement model to make changes in your life. Section 5 identifies 10 dimensions of daily living. When you determine you are ready for change, the quality improvement model provides a systematic method to obtain your intended outcome. Armed with information about change theory; quality improvement models; and technological and non-technological tools, let's get into the heart of the material to demonstrate how you can find your time.

Section 5 – Using Time to Manage Life Dimensions

An individual has many factors to consider as they live their life. These factors take time and often repeat needed activities daily, weekly or annually. These factors, or dimensions, fall into 10 categories: health, food, household maintenance, travel, finances, work, education, hobbies, service opportunities, and relationship building. Life dimensions are similar to the nine systems that need to function in the human body in order to sustain life. Just like the body systems, the life dimensions interact, vying for the time and attention of the individual. A person in modern society does not live in isolation and cannot be comfortable interacting with only the dimensions of his own life, he must also interact with others who are dealing with the dynamics of their life dimensions. These interactions become the glue that holds families, communities, and the world together.

Morgenstern conducted an informal survey of her website visitors, asking why they wanted to become better time managers. She found that "more than 70 percent of fifteen hundred respondents said they wanted to find more time."[19] An individual has many demands on his day regarding how he spends his time. Trying to separate any dimension of his life and isolating it from the whole person is impossible.

A woman with small children working in a job outside the home is the ultimate multi-tasking guru as she juggles herself through life – trying to keep all relevant issues under control and moving along. Allen discusses the needed control in juggling her tasks from both a horizontal and vertical perspective.[20] He explains horizontal control as thinking needed to "maintain coherence across all activities" that her job outside the home and caring for her children require. Vertical control focuses thinking on a project, specifically, such as making a speech at a conference or taking a child to the doctor. A great analogy is a pilot flying an airplane. As he flies the airplane, it is important that the pilot have vertical control. Vertical control includes those things required to fly an airplane, like checking that the engines are working, making sure there is gas in the airplane, and the radios are capturing the instructions by the tower. However, the pilot must also fly horizontally, that is, high enough not to hit the trees while thinking about the landing.

Sandie Barrie

Horizontal and vertical controls provide direction in managing life dimensions and neither cannot work alone. Horizontal control maintains evenness across all the dimensions in your life, which is finding time to be able to exercise and get the children off to school, as well as balancing your life dimensions with the life dimensions of others. Vertical control provides us with the ability to concentrate on a specific situation within a life dimension. Each life dimension is interrelated with the rest of the life dimensions. As the pilot must have both vertical and horizontal control to fly safely, so must you balance *between* your life dimensions as well as *within* your life dimensions and *between* the life dimensions of those with whom you live and work.

Balance is something we all work toward from the days we learned to walk up to now, as we struggle to keep everything working and moving in the direction of happiness for ourselves, our families, and the world in which we live.

In Section 5, the discussion proceeds to examine the 10 life dimensions from a vertical control perspective – that is, we will examine specific situations within each of the life dimensions. Later, in Section 6, the discussion focuses on strategies to keep the 10 life dimensions working together from a horizontal control perspective within you and between others in your life. This discussion starts with exploring the most important dimension in your life, which is your health.

Health is a broad topic! Applying the quality improvement model to the health dimension finds many situations for applications. Let's start with personal health. First, you need to <u>assess</u> your personal health by <u>asking</u> yourself some questions. Then, after doing some research, you develop a <u>plan</u> to improve personal health, find strategies to <u>do</u> the plan, and using a check sheet to collect data, identify how to <u>check</u> progress through analysis of performance indicators, and finally, <u>review</u> the overall progress over time. In the review component, you evaluate what stage of change you have obtained, whether it is maintenance, where effective change occurs with few to no relapses, or termination, because change has occurred. The review component and your ability to do and redo the quality improvement model repeatedly until the outcome occurs is the most important point for you to consider!

Find Your Time: Assess, Plan, Do, Check, Review

Each life dimension has many situations that present for opportunities for using the quality improvement model. Three situations in each life dimension demonstrates how the quality improvement model works. As you regularly use the quality improvement in your life, Appendix B provides additional situations for each life dimension where you can find your time and thus enjoy your life more.

The examples presented intentionally start with health, since having your health is key to being able to spend the time needed to utilize the quality improvement model in your life. There are many situations for the dimension of health. The three situations presented here use the quality improvement model to improve your weight, manage chronic pain, and establish a home medical record.

Health

Health is more than just the absence of disease. Physical health refers to health of the body. Mental health refers to health of the mind. Our personal health encompasses both and is basic to life. Many of us have experienced at least a short episode of illness. You understand that when you are sick you cannot enjoy life. Many of us take our health for granted until a major life event occurs. Such events could be as simple as neck or hip pain, or more complex as developing sleep apnea.

Sandie Barrie

Improving Your Weight

A few basic questions provide an overview of how you perceive what is important in the dimension of your life related to health.

Assess

- How much time do you spend working on your personal health?
- How much do you weigh?
- How tall are you?
- How does your weight compare to your body mass index?
- What type of exercise do you do?
- How much exercise do you do?
- How many calories do you take in per day?
- Do you have any health issues such as: depression, diabetes, high blood pressure, or sleep apnea, where weight is a causative or contributing factor to the disease?
- If so, do you understand what is going wrong and how you can correct the condition or disease process? In addition, if not corrected, do you understand how you can keep the problem(s) from getting worse?
- Have you seen a physician in the last year for a check-up?

Plan

There is so much information available to you today especially on how you can improve or maintain your health. This is a great area to start out simply. While your plan could have many goals and objectives, let's start by focusing again on weight. Weigh yourself on a dependable scale. Stand up next to a wall and have a friend mark straight across at the top of your head to measure your height. These two numbers will allow you to determine your body mass index (BMI).

The BMI is a widely used measurement that compares your height and weight to calculate an estimate of body fat. The National Institute of Health provides a calculator on their website at http://www.nhlbisupport.com/bmi/bmicalc.htm. All you have to do is enter your weight and height and you will see where you fall on the scale from underweight to obesity. Now you can see what your ideal goal weight should be.

To gain or lose weight is simply a combination of how much food you eat and how much you exercise. First, let's do some research on food, and then exercise.

Food consists of carbohydrates (sugars), fats, and proteins, but one thing most foods have are calories. Oh, that word! A calorie indicates a unit of food energy. Digestion uses calories. So now, you need to determine how many calories you need daily to maintain your weight, reduce your weight, or increase your weight. Nevertheless, before we do that, let's look at exercise and determine how much activity you get in a day.

There are four exercise categories: sedentary (not able to exercise, little to no physical activity, usually sits or lies all day); light exercise or activity; moderate exercise or activity; or heavy exercise or activity. Be honest with yourself.

Go to the Calorie Control Council's website at http://www.caloriecontrol.org/calcalcs.html . Here you will be able to put in your height, weight, age, and activity level. Then you will be able to determine the daily calories to maintain or improve your weight. I found that I could have 1574.3 calories a day. Even more interesting is to go to your favorite fast food website and see how many calories are in your favorite meal. I found that there are 540 calories in my favorite salad at Wendy's.

Now that you have done some research and taken a few calculations, you are ready to set out a plan. You have a better picture of the range of weight you need to be in, as well how many calories you should take in daily and how much exercise you need to do to gain, maintain, or lose weight. You are in charge and you can see what needs to occur.

Again, this book is not about motivating you on to change or maintain your weight. Nevertheless, if you want something to occur, like losing weight, you will have to do something, or you may just keep adding weight to your frame, as you get older. It only takes a few minutes to write down a goal and objective(s) to start the process. Once these two elements are completed, it becomes much easier to develop the performance indicator(s).

<u>Goal - long range:</u>

Get to body mass index of 24.8 by decreasing weight to 127 pounds within six months

<u>Objective(s) - future condition(s):</u>

- Decrease current weight of 137 pounds by two pounds every four weeks by cutting down on my food portions and increasing my exercise:
  - Prepare Jell-O, fruit salad and celery stalks and always have them ready and available to eat in refrigerator;
  - Have chicken noodle soup and crackers for lunch five out of seven days;
  - Eat breakfast at 6 a.m., lunch at 11 a.m. and supper at 6 p.m. daily; limit snacks to 100 calories in mid-afternoon and prior to going to bed, and
  - Walk around the block four days each week.

<u>Performance Indicator(s) - current condition(s):</u>

- Current weight by month
- Current BMI by month

Do

In Section 3, a similar check sheet provided an example on collecting data.

Check

In addition, the check component is similar to the example used in Section 3. Many people have problems with taking their weight. They may take their weight frequently. On the other hand, they may never get on the scale. They often keep the "magic number" in their head rather than writing it down Finally, adding two indicators, current BMI and current weight, to the performance indicators dashboard (see Appendix A) will allow you to monitor progress while you are working on your change, and then to maintain the change – in this case, when the goal weight has been obtained.

Review

When the review period comes up, hopefully, in this case, you will be jumping for joy as you determine that you are closer to your goal. This is the important point, if you have not reached your goal, put the quality improvement model into play again. Go back to the first component, "assess," and ask yourself a series of new questions or simply review the original set of questions.

By evaluating your performance indicators for health periodically, you can make adjustments as needed, either continuing on with your current eating and exercise habits, or reviewing your previous plan to determine whether it is working for you or whether new strategies and tactics need to be put in place.

Time Management Outcome – Find Your Time by Improving Your Weight

A year down the road, weight has been lost. You have reached your BMI goal. You have changed your lifestyle. However, stop for a minute and calculate the time you saved by not having to research how to lose weight, the doctor appointments avoided because less disease has taken over, and less time trying to fit into the skinny jeans that now fit!

Sandie Barrie

Managing Chronic Pain

The second situation examined within the health dimension is managing chronic pain. Many suffer from chronic pain, which robs hours and days from their life. Learning how to manage chronic pain can contribute markedly to grabbing stolen time back.

Assess

- How much time do you spend in pain on a daily basis?
- Do you understand why you have pain?
- Have you had diagnostic tests to help you understand what is causing the pain?
- Are you doing anything to manage your pain?
- Are the strategies you are using working?
- Do you want to learn new strategies for living without pain that don't require you to take heavy medications?

Plan

The volume of material available on chronic pain and pain management are wide and varied. The WebMD Website has an excellent guide that helps one understand pain and how to manage it. You can find it at http://www.webmd.com/pain-management/guide/pain-management-overview-facts. In studying this website, you will find information about a myriad of causes for pain. It is easy to speculate on what is causing the pain. First, determine the frequency, duration, and intensity of the pain by taking a few measurements. It is important to record what you did to try and get pain relief – say, taking some medications, lying down to rest, or getting a massage. Write a broad goal and then write objectives that support the goal.

Goal - long range:

- Reduce neck pain

Objective(s) – future condition(s):

- To increase the number of pain-free days by evaluating pain relief strategies
- To reduce frequency of daily pain in the neck
- To reduce duration of each episode of daily pain in the neck
- To reduce intensity of each episode of daily pain in the neck

Performance Indicator(s) - current condition(s):

- Number of pain-free days by month

Do

Taking some measurements for a short period will give you information about when you are having pain and what works or does not work to relieve the pain. See Table 3 - Daily Pain Monitoring Tool below.

Table 3 - Daily Pain Monitoring Tool

Date: Monday				
Hour of Day	Frequency Did I have pain during the following hour? Where?	Relief Strategies What did I do to relieve the pain? Medication, lie down, massage?	Intensity How bad was the pain? (Scale of 1 to 10 with 1 being a little pain and 10 being worst pain I have ever felt)	Duration How long did pain last in minutes?
Midnight				
1				
2				
3	√ neck pain	medication	7	60
4	√ neck pain		4	60
5	√ neck pain		3	15
6				
7				
8				
9				
10				
11				
Noon				
1				
2				
3				
4	√ neck pain	medication	7	60
5	√ neck pain		5	60
6	√ neck pain		4	15
7			sleep	
8	√ neck pain		3	15
9				
10				
11				

Check

In analyzing the five data collection sheets, using medication occurred on days that I had pain (only one check sheet included). Relief from pain occurred on each day. The medication consisted of muscle relaxants and synthetic codeine. I desired a strategy without using medications. Okay now I have determine with data collection what is working and not working as I try to manage the pain experienced by my body. I can determine what strategies might work to get off the medication. The information collected on which strategies work or don't work is very important to take with you when you visit your physician.

Review

The review component of the quality improvement model is very important, especially if the chronic pain is recurring. If you need to talk with your doctor, talk with him. If you need an advocate when you talk to the doctor, take someone with you to help you say what you need to say. With time and persistence, you can determine why you have chronic pain and how to get out of the pain.

> **Time Management Outcome – Find Your Time by Managing Chronic Pain**
>
> Think about the last time you had an experience with chronic pain and what you could have done with the time you spent trying to get rid of the chronic pain. Avoiding or controlling the pain that comes with age and/or disease can occur when relaxation techniques and exercise occur. Spending some of your time to determine what is causing the pain is time well spent.

Establishing a Home Medical Record

The third situation to find your time within the health life dimension is in establishing a home medical record. One of the lines in Tom Daschle's book, *Critical: What We Can Do About the Health Crisis* says it all, "Trying to navigate the (health care) system can be like taking a multiple-choice exam in a subject you've never studied."[21] In the previous example, the focus centered around chronic pain. Almost everyone knows the health care delivery system in this country is broken and one place that there are serious issues is in dealing with the paperwork associated with personal medical records. Medical records are the specific documents that follow the patient as they move through the system and receive care. The paperwork can be very confusing, is often lost, and is frequently not available to the physician who is evaluating the needs of individuals to improve their health.

Assess

- How much time do you spend maintaining your home medical records?
- Do you have any records of blood tests, x-ray reports, or other health information?
- Have you placed all the information in one place?
- Have you taken the time to organize the material?
- Do you understand what the reports are saying about you?

Plan

While many people in this country obtain their health care from a system that has computerized medical records, most do not have the advantage of having their records available to all the physicians that may be treating them. The plan is simple making health information available to anyone, who is interested in saving time and having information about their health available to the physicians and other providers who are caring for them. You can obtain a copy of any piece of data that is collected when you visit your doctor or have a procedure or surgery completed. See the following website at http://www.hhs.gov/ocr/privacy/hipaa/understanding/consumers/index.html that describes the rules that apply to the Health Insurance Portability and Accountability Act of 1996 (HIPAA). Briefly, you will have to sign a release form to gain the document.

You may not need every single piece of health data collected on you. However, when a major procedure or surgery is completed obtaining the results and placing them into your home medical record should occur. The results of a previous MRI may provide valuable information to your current doctor as he compares the old MRI to one done recently. Even as we move toward eventually having computerized medical records, it will be impossible to collect all the relevant paper from all your doctors prior to its implementation. The full implementation across the country will take anywhere from five to 10 years to accomplish. Therefore, here is a goal and some objectives.

Goal - long range:

- Maintain a home medical record

Objective(s) - future condition(s):

- Be able to locate lab results completed
- Be able to locate x-ray results completed
- Be able to identify medications taken during the year

Performance Indicator (current condition):

- Copy of updated home medical records by month

Do

Make a simple medical record for home use by taking a manila folder and punching two holes at the top of both pages. Open up the folder and on the left side complete a form similar to "Your Health Journal" promulgated by the Joint Commission and available at http://utility2.realage.com/media/pdfs/SP_HealthJournal.pdf. Completing the journal will provide both general and specific information relevant to your health status.

Take all the health data on yourself and place it into three categories: (1) notes from physicians, (2) medication information sheets that accompany prescription drugs, and (3) test reports (x-rays, laboratory data, and MRIs). Punch holes at the top of all the physician notes and place on the file fastener that you have hooked to the right side at the top of the manila folder. Place a colored sheet of paper on top of the physician notes and then place the medication information sheets on top and then another colored piece of paper and then the test reports on top. Always file the most recent document on top in the appropriate section. If the file becomes unmanageable, separate the file into additional manila folders. Make a separate home medical record for your spouse and for each child, and/or for others that you are helping manage their health care.

Additionally, make a separate folder for insurance papers and resource data that you have obtained. Be sure to date any resource material so that you know how old the information is when you pull out the file to refer to it. Place your file folder and the file folders of the others that you are managing into a file cabinet where you can easily get to it should you need it quickly.

Check

Every month, place a date on your calendar to review your home medical record to ensure that you have included all pertinent data from the previous month. In addition, once a year, ask your pharmacy to print out your medication report so that you have a record for years to come as to what medication you have taken during the year. In doing analysis, comparing when you made a visit to a health care provider and whether you have any documentation becomes important. Even after signing HIPAA forms, you have to monitor whether the documents arrive. You may have to call a second time to get the copy desired. This is important since filing papers into a home medical record file may not be high on your priority list when you are dealing with a sick child or have just returned from Urgent Care with an elderly parent.

Review

Annually, take the home medical record file with you when you go to your primary care doctor so you can be sure that they are aware of all things that have occurred. If you have an accident, or a significant health event where you are unconscious, and you have shared where your home medical record is with the rest of your family, they will be able to get it and bring it to the hospital for the doctors to have access. It is also a great idea to take and make a full copy of the home medical record and put it into a secure space like a safety deposit box to ensure that you have a copy in case you lose your original or some catastrophe causes destruction to the paper file. You can also scan the documents and place the files on a disk or a thumb drive making the storage process less cumbersome and easier if you should desire to keep your medical records with you as you travel.

> **Time Management Outcome – Find Your Time by Establishing a Home Medical Record**
>
> When you receive your laboratory results from this year and you have educated yourself on what the values mean, you will be able to compare the results from last year. You will not have to waste time trying to determine where you placed last year's report.
>
> Take your medical record, when you have to go to the Urgent Care so the strange doctor can understand your unique situation with the chronic conditions you have. You can quickly pull the file from the cabinet as you grab your car keys.
>
> If you desire to travel and have known serious medical conditions, having your home medical record with you will be a time saver if you should have to seek medical attention, especially if you or your loved ones are not able to provide details about your medical conditions. The doctor will not have to try to call your primary care physician in another part of the country with different time zones and conflicting office hours.

In summary, see Appendix A for a table that demonstrates how one can monitor performance indicators by month for the health dimension. While you can use Microsoft Word 2003 or Microsoft Excel 2003 to develop this form, paper and pencil will accomplish the same goal of recording information on a monthly basis. Appendix B provides additional situations for the health dimension you can explore using the quality improvement model to make changes you desire in your life. The Selected Resources Section provides reference materials to help you as you develop your plan. Now having gotten your health dimension in order let us move onto another important dimension of your life, food.

Food

As you know, we cannot survive without food. Consequently, the topic of food provides a major opportunity for a person to examine how he spends his time. Using the quality improvement model, the three situations presented for the food dimension include: making good choices about where to eat; doing meal preparation and cleanup; and organizing for purchasing groceries and household items. For the most part, people buy their food and then prepare it. However, a growing number purchase their meals at restaurants. Let's start with where to eat.

Making Good Choices About Where to Eat

Last night, I simply did not want to cook supper, so I asked my husband if we could go out to eat. I have been making evening meals for more years than I can remember – first, for my family of origin, and then for my husband and children, and now, just for my husband and me. Over the years, the number of times in any given week that I cooked versus the times we went out to eat in a restaurant has vacillated. My family of origin never went out to eat in restaurants. I can remember my first dates with my husband where going to a local restaurant near Grant Park, IL, was seriously a new venture. My husband and I frequently worked opposite shifts while our family was growing and so we did not go out to restaurants often. Later, as the children grew older, we had conflicting schedules, and the children started to have minds of their own when it came to what they wanted to eat, we succumbed to eating more and more at restaurants. This habit continued after our children left our home and my husband and I continued in high-powered jobs. It simply seemed easier to eat out. Now, as retirement becomes a reality, budget constraints have us eating more and more at home. Oftentimes, I have found myself thinking that eating out has us consume more calories than we need, costs more than we want to pay, and takes a lot more time than it would for me to prepare our food at home.

Assess

- Do you do advance planning as to where you will consume your food during the week?
- Looking over the last month, how many meals have you eaten at home and how many meals have you eaten at a restaurant?
- How much money have you spent on groceries for consumption in the home and how much have you spent when eating out?

Plan

As you look at the questions in the assessment section, most of us probably do not have data on this topic. We simply know that you eat some of your meals at home and you eat some of your meals at restaurants. For the purposes of looking at this situation, the discussion will focus on where we eat, and for those meals eaten outside of the home, we will examine why we ate meals away from our homes.

It is interesting to look at guesstimating the numbers of meals that you prepare and eat at home versus the number of meals that you eat at restaurants. There are arguments pro and con for eating at home versus eating at a restaurant. Our purpose here is not to complete a criticism for one way or the other. There are a myriad of reasons why someone might look at eating at one place or another that take into consideration such factors as time, cost, and calories.

For the purpose of our discussion, let's look at the person who has decided that she believes it takes more time to go out to restaurants in her area and that it costs more to eat out than it does to eat at home. Emily wants to decrease the number of times she eats out at restaurants and to understand what the purpose is for the meals she eats at restaurants. Emily has a variety of reasons that conflict with her basic desire to eat at home, such as, working an eight-hour shift where she needs to eat away from home, a big family that wants to go out often to celebrate different functions, and she just *likes* to eat at Black Rock Pizza. She knows that she will continue to eat meals outside of her home, but she would like to decrease the total number each month because she believes she will gain time in the process and save money. She writes a goal, some objectives, and performance indicators.

Goal - long range

- Reduce number of meals that are eaten outside of the home

Objective(s) - future condition(s):

- Eat 90% of meals at home
- Be able to determine the purpose of each meal eaten away from home

Performance Indicator(s) - current condition(s):

- Number of meals eaten at home by month
- Number of meals eaten in restaurants by month
- Number of meals by purpose eaten outside of home by month

Do

A simple data collection sheet will help Emily determine when and why she is eating meals away from her home. Table 4 below provides data for where Emily ate her food for one month.

Table 4 – Data Collection Home Versus Restaurant

	Month: February					
	Eating at Home			Eating at Restaurant		
	B	L	S	B	L	S
1	√	√	√			
2	√		√		√	
3	√		√		√	
4	√				√	√ new job
5			√	√ meeting	√	
6	√		√		√	
7	√	√	√			
8	√	√				√ meeting
9	√		√		√	
10	√				√	√ friends
11	√		√		√	
12			√	√ meeting	√	
13	√				√	√ friends
14	√	√	√			
15	√	√	√			
16	√		√		√	
17	√				√	√ friends
18	√		√		√	
19			√	√ meeting	√	
20	√				√	√ friends
21	√	√				√ friends
22	√	√	√			
23	√		√		√	
24	√		√		√	
25	√				√	√ friends
26				√ meeting	√	√ friends
27	√				√	√ friends
28	√	√	√ friends			
Total	24	8	18	4	20	10

Check

Analysis is easy. For the month of February, Emily ate 59.5% of her meals at home. When it comes time to evaluate where Emily's ate her food for the month, we find she ate most breakfast meals at home except on Thursdays when Emily went to the weekly meeting with her fellow employees. She ate lunches out at the local restaurants during the workweek, rotating to a different restaurant each day. She ate nine supper meals with friends and family to celebrate events or just to talk. Of the 18 supper meals eaten at home, Emily only had one meal where she had friends eat with her. Again, the purpose here is to see that it is easy to collect data on a topic of interest.

Review

Once Emily had data on whether she ate a restaurant or not and the purpose of eating at the restaurant, she was able to analyze the data and make determinations about where she can make changes. If Emily's goal is to reduce the number of meals she eats in restaurants and she has not accomplished the goal, she can set new goals. She can bring her lunch to work and eat at her desk, or she might start asking her friends to her home to eat rather than going out to restaurants. Emily asked me where we were going to celebrate my birthday this year. We decided to have the party at my house. We did not have to make a reservation. We did not have to stand in line to wait for a table big enough for the 12 people that gathered to celebrate. We did not have to leave in a hurry. Moreover, because we used the money to buy food for a dinner at my house, which we were able to do at a lower cost, we were able to have lots of family and friends attend. It sure was a fun night!

Find Your Time: Assess, Plan, Do, Check, Review

> **Time Management Outcome – Find Your Time by Making Good Choices About Where To Eat**
>
> Taking time to determine whether to eat out at a restaurant or eat in at home depends on individual circumstances. The important point is determining whether you are using your time wisely when it comes to taking in your food. Eating is a social activity. It is an activity that is necessary for life and one that we do every day. Make a right decision to avoid wasting time whether it is by eating at home or eating at a restaurant. The decision is yours to make. Make the right choice and you may not only save time, you may find that you could be spending on an activity that you prefer. You may find that you are eating a meal with fewer calories which saves you time on the treadmill.

Doing Meal Preparation and Clean-Up

In 1962, at 6 p.m., my family sat down at the table – all 15 of us – for supper! As I think back, the food was simple. After grace, we each took turns passing the food to the right. I never learned about "leftovers" because if there were any scraps, our beloved dog Radar got them. Can you imagine doing meal preparation? In addition, we did it every night! We did not go out to restaurants. McDonald's was just not popular. We did not get to roam the kitchen and raid the refrigerator, either, so we were hungry when we sat down to eat. Mom was the chief cook, but she did have many assistants. Around 4:30 p.m., even today, I start thinking about what it is that I am going to serve for supper, which occurs routinely at 6 p.m. Some things just don't change.

Even more fun, as I recall, was preparing lunch buckets for each of us as we all tried to get our breakfast. We generally got a sandwich, some potato chips, and a cupcake. While I was in grade school, there were no school lunches, which changed when I got to high school.

Sandie Barrie

Breakfast was a bowl of cereal and milk from the five-gallon containers the milkman brought to our house twice a week.

Our mom must have done cleanup after we all left for school because our kitchen was always clean when we got home from school. Clean-up after the supper meal was left to the girls in the family, and my sister Ronnie has great stories about us doing that together – me washing and her drying the dishes since there were no paper plates.

Assess

- How much time do you spend on meal preparation?
- Who does the meal preparation in your family?
- Do you own and use a freezer?
- Do you make batches of food?
- Do you buy your groceries for the next meal on your way home from work?
- What process do you have for cleaning up after the meal?

Plan

Meal preparation need not be fancy. It makes sense to think about what we are going to serve for the evening meal early in the day, especially if you are the one who makes the meal. Meal planning is not something I have done on a regular basis, however, my son plans out with his family (a total of four) what they are going to eat for the week, buys the groceries, and cooks the evening meal six out of seven days per week. There are several tools on the Internet to assist with the process of planning meals and cleaning up afterward. One-time tested and yet still relevant reference is *Betty Crocker's Cookbook: Everything You Need to Know to Cook Today*[22]. You can visit at http://www.bettycrocker.com/store/.

<u>Goal - long range:</u>

- Plan meals for next week and cleanup after each meal this week

Objective(s) - future condition(s):

- Identify preferences of food for those eating at home
- Discuss with family meals for next week, identifying any unusual situations
- Prepare grocery list prior to going to grocery store
- Determine who will do and when cleanup after meals will occur

Performance Indicator(s) - current condition(s):

- Number of time wasters identified in food preparation and cleanup by month
- Family satisfaction with meal preparation by month
- Family satisfaction with cleanup by month

Do

Just last week, my husband and I had a server at a restaurant ask us to complete a survey on her food serving performance on the Internet so she could keep her number-one spot. I don't see food surveys at my house – after 42 years of fixing meals for my husband, I know what he likes and dislikes. He is a wise man – he eats what I serve. However, in the interest of the quality improvement model, a simple question at the end of the meal is appropriate for the cook to ask whether those eating liked the dishes served that night. For no matter how you look at it, if people are not satisfied with the food prepared, they will not eat it or they will complain.

The one thing that I do that helps with cleanup is that after washing my hands prior to starting the meal preparation, I fill the sink with very hot water. As I prepare the food, I place dirty dishes into the hot water. Hot sudsy water is a great bath for the dishes as they come off the table.

Sandie Barrie

Check

Knowing what I like and what my husband likes, I am able to go to the grocery store and buy food for the next month and make appropriate purchases and life moves on. Determining what people like to eat and planning out to some degree what I am going to cook each night earlier in the day lets me have more time to do other things I like to do.

Review

Stop and think just for a minute – what does your kitchen look like right now? Are you pleased with the picture you see or do you want some changes? Using the quality improvement model allows you to focus overall on the process of food preparation, or a component of it, from deciding what to buy, where to buy it, whether to purchase food in bulk, whether to use coupons, deciding to prepare food in advance, or assigning the cleanup. There are many opportunities to take the time wasters out, to make mealtime a relaxing experience, and to go to bed with the dishes done.

Time Management Outcome – Find Your Time by Doing Meal Preparation and Clean-up

For over 50 years, I have made at least one meal (and for many days of my life two meals) for myself and one other person (mostly my husband). So how many days have I been cooking meals? Assuming that I started cooking for my family when I was 10, and that I ate from hospital cafeterias for three years while I was in nursing school, let's see if we do the math (50 years x 365 days = 21,250 days).

The fun part starts when one adds up all the hours surrounding getting the food to the table. Wow, this certainly must lead to a Ph.D., in something because if, for every meal, one hour is spent, that's 21,250 hours. Even more interesting is converting the 21,250 hours to the number of workweeks in a year. Wait, I have to get the calculator: 21,250 divided by 2,080 is 10 WORK YEARS! Yikes – that is a lot of time from Monday through Friday, 9 to 5, for 10 years. How many hours do you have in food preparation and cleanup?

You can find time as you review the system and processes you have established as they relate to food preparation and cleanup. Many of us follow simple routines that we have been doing repeatedly for years without much thought of what we could do differently. Exploring how we perform the tasks related to food preparation and cleanup can provide us with many opportunities to save time. In addition, if you are a recipient of someone else's food preparation and cleanup, consider yourself a lucky person.

Organizing for Purchasing Groceries and Household Items

One of the more time-consuming elements of food preparation is the purchasing of the groceries and other items needed to run a household. I just went to the store and realized I forgot to purchase something. For me, the trip back to the store is only minutes away.

Sandie Barrie

However, the traffic, standing in line again, and the general fatigue that comes with shopping will all be repeated because I forgot something I needed to buy. Of course, many things are wants, not needs. Today, I needed a can of tomatoes for the meatloaf I'm making for my birthday party tonight.

As I sit here typing out the text, I recall how my mom got groceries for our family. We lived in the country and times were different. If we ran out of something, we would walk up the long road and ask the neighbor for a couple of eggs or a cup of sugar. My dad hunted in the woods around our house, we had a large garden, and we canned a lot of our food during the summers in preparation for the winters. My mom had the luxury of not going to grocery stores. However, of course, even in 1962, we needed some items that came from the grocery store. Therefore, every couple of weeks, my mom wrote out a grocery list, called up the grocer at the Big Bear in Kankakee, IL, and the employees gathered the food into a grocery cart and wheeled across the street to my dad's floral shop. He put the groceries in his vehicle and brought them home to a waiting wife who put her order away. Moreover, there was no charge for gathering and delivering the groceries, as there is today.

Assess

- How frequently do you purchase groceries and household items?
- How many stores do you go when buying groceries?
- Do you work from a list or from memory?
- How many times do you go to the store each week?
- Are you aware of the sales and coupons used by stores that you frequent?

Plan

Most of us do not plan for how we get our food into our homes. We just stop by the store once or twice a week and purchase what it is we think we need for the next few days or we get something we see that we want to eat. Our goal here is to look at the amount of time you spend purchasing food and other items and to determine whether reducing the number of trips to the grocery store will save you some time.

Goal - long range:

- Reduce the amount of time spent on purchasing groceries and household items

Objective(s) - future condition(s):

- Prepare a master list of grocery and household items
- Determine the best place to purchase the items listed on master list

Performance Indicator(s) - current condition(s):

- Number of extra trips required to purchase groceries/household items by month

Do

Mom used a scrap of paper to write down what she wanted before she placed the order over the phone. I have never used a list to remember what I wanted to purchase from the grocery store. I simply walk up and down each store aisle and tick items off in my head – got plenty of soap, don't need sugar, and almost out of tea, so let's put in the cart.

Another approach is to have a master grocery list. In my research for this book, I found several websites that provide free-of-charge printable grocery lists. I also found that these sites offer printable coupons on products, which was a little bit of a distraction since I was really trying to find ways to save time on the purchasing component of food preparation. What I really wanted was a list by aisle of articles I wanted to purchase, and by store, with the best price (with or without a coupon). Then, if I could get someone else to go and do the purchasing once a month, I would just have to put it away. Therefore, I decided to examine several of the websites available. The Google search brought up several for me to review. Once I got the list of items, I then put together my own master grocery list for the three local stores: Walmart, Costco, and a regional grocery store. I organized the list by aisle and by frequency of purchase. This was an important point since it helps me remember what I purchased and how often – whether it be once a week or once a year.

Check

I cannot tell you how many times I have stopped for just one or two items at a grocery store on my way home. While I was working, I never took the time to analyze my process of shopping for groceries and household items. For me, since I purchase everything that comes into our home, I need to get my husband to review the list before I go shopping once a month (for the major purchases) to see if there is something he needs. He seems to remember that he needs one item one day and another item the next day.

Checking my system once a month, I have refined it. I purchase all paper goods once a year, including detergent, shampoo, and cleaning supplies. I purchase meat once a month and freeze it in one-meal portions, and thaw it easily in the microwave when it comes time to prepare the food. In addition, I get staples like rice, salad dressings, and canned foods once a month. Once a week, I shop for perishables – milk, fruits, and veggies. I realized that as I started to eat more meals at home, I needed to plan for the functions (like birthday parties) that I was going to have at my house rather than go out to a restaurant to celebrate.

Review

Take time to look at how you purchase food for you and your family. It might be vastly different depending on what part of the country you live in, how many people you are cooking for, and what your financial resources are. While the system works for my husband and me, we will have to revisit our strategies as we age or if someone moves into our home with us.

The day will come when I will swipe the bar code on each item that I use when I prepare my meals and then an automatic grocery list will be developed and sent to the store where the best bargains are on sale for the week. An automatic system will deduct the amount from my bank account and all I will have to do is open the door and receive the delivery of goods. Even in Sparks, NV, you can now order groceries online and go pick them up. It is a service that you have to pay for, and the regional grocery store providing the service costs are the highest! Life is all about trade-offs.

Therefore, for now, I will continue to take the time to get my own groceries. It is great to know that things are coming full circle and that my mom was way ahead of the time when she placed an order at the Big Bear close to 50 years ago.

> **Time Management Outcome – Find Your Time by Organizing for Purchasing Groceries and Household Items**
>
> Knowing that I can go to my kitchen and prepare tonight's meal for anywhere from one to 15 people without going to the grocery store is comforting. I know that if my sons call and need me to watch the grandchildren and cook them a meal, I can do it. The fun continues for me to be able to reduce the time needed to get the food that my husband and I need to an even lower number of hours by determining what else I can cut out of the process to get the food from the environment to my kitchen table without paying extra to have it done.

In summary, see Appendix A for a table that demonstrates how one can monitor performance indicators by month for the food dimension. While you can use Microsoft Word 2003 or Microsoft Excel 2003 to develop this form, paper and pencil will accomplish the same goal of recording information on a monthly basis. Appendix B provides additional situations for the food dimension where you can explore using the quality improvement model to make changes you desire in your life. The Selected Resources Section provides reference materials to help you as you develop your plan. Now having gotten our food dimension in order, let us move onto another important dimension of our lives, household maintenance.

Sandie Barrie

Household Maintenance

Back to my family of origin – we lived in a small house on the Iroquois River in Kankakee, Il. In 1946, my dad built our first home. My dad brought out a room from the greenhouse that my dad's family owned. My dad built two other rooms around it. My dad added two bedrooms as our family grew. This is where my family of origin lived our lives. For all of us, life goes on in our homes. Using the quality improvement model, three situations are reviewed in the household maintenance dimension: recycling daily, reducing time spent doing laundry, and taking pictures of possessions.

Recycling Daily

We eat in our homes. We bathe in our homes. We sleep in our homes. We entertain in our homes. All these activities generate trash: boxes, cans and glass, plastic bags, and other garbage. Packaging did not include plastic in food packaging, when I was growing up, and during the early years of my marriage. Everything came in a box or a can. My mom disposed of the paper by burning most of it in the fire pit, as did most of the rest of our neighbors. She took the cans to a dump in the back of our property. Today, I live in Sparks, NV, and you wouldn't think of burning your trash. There is a lot more plastic. Every item purchased must be put in a plastic or paper bag to get it out of the store with only a few exceptions. As the week goes by, I simply put the garbage into waste containers that I have in every room of the house. Then, once a week, a garbage truck comes and picks up the trash.

Assess

- What do you do with the waste that you generate in your life?
- Do you recycle any items?
- Does your family want to assist in the process?
- Who takes out the trash in your home?

Plan

We have been hearing about global warming for a number of years and since I retired from my day job, I thought, *Okay I can do this.* Therefore, I called up the waste management folks and asked them for some of the green and yellow recycling containers that my neighbors were using. I learned that glass goes in the green container and plastic and cans go in the yellow container.

Goal - long range:

- Recycle the garbage that is generated in my home

Objective(s) - future condition(s):

- To increase the number of times plastic, glass and cans are put in the yellow and green bins and taken to the curb for pick-up
- To increase the number of times that discarded computer paper is put in the paper bag and taken to the curb for pick-up
- To increase the number of plastic bags that are returned to Walmart
- To increase the number of discarded items that are taken to nonprofit organizations

Performance Indicator(s) - current condition(s):

- Number of times plastic, glass, cans, and discarded computer paper were recycled per month
- Number of times plastic bags were returned to Walmart per month

Do

I had to change a few behaviors. Instead of turning to the right to put the cans into the trash bin, I had to turn to the left and put the item in the box I placed under the sink. At first, I was taking the recyclables to the green and yellow containers in the garage that was down a few sets of stairs. That got old very fast. Therefore, I placed a box under the sink where I can place the recycled items. I then just have to empty the kitchen box into the appropriate green and yellow containers once a week and put the containers out to the curb every two weeks on Friday before the recycling truck comes. I had to put a box under the printer table so as a piece of non-confidential paper came off the computer that I didn't need, I could put it into the box. I had to designate a place in the garage that I would place all the plastic bags as I got home and unloaded the groceries. I also had to take the discarded computer paper from under the printer and place it in a brown bag and put out to the curb for pick-up.

Check

The name of the game is to make recycling easy, mindless. So now instead of putting the plastic, cans, or glass into the trash receptacle, I place them under the sink in the box for recycled items. On trash day, I place the recycled items into the proper bins and put at the curbside for pick-up. I did have to put a reminder in my Microsoft Outlook 2003 Calendar to remind me to put the recycling bins out at the curb. As changes go, this one went fast and now I can brag that I recycle.

Review

I have cans, plastic containers, and glass under control. I will be starting to move toward thinking about how I discard other items that I no longer want, most of which go to the local nonprofit organizations for resale. One thing that I have decided to do is to share how easy this process is with other people when the topic of recycling comes up, so maybe I will be able to influence someone else in my life to recycle.

> ### Time Management Outcome – Find Your Time Recycling Daily
>
> Recycling is about managing the time you spend discarding garbage. Perhaps it will be just making a left turn instead of making a right turn when you discard items. Twenty minutes a month can make a small contribution in making the world a better place to live. Just think, if we all made this small change, we might be able to make a dent in the global warming issue. In addition, we could spend less time listening to commercials and stories about recycling. When you realize how you spend your time, it helps you not only find your time but also to use your time wisely.

Reducing Time Spent Doing Laundry

Years ago, doing the laundry was a time-intensive process, as generally, the woman of the house placed the clothes in a wringer washing machine, carried the laundry outside, and hung the clothes on the clothesline with clothespins. The process took all day – or several days – depending on how many people lived in the household. We must clean the clothes we wear. Taking the time to evaluate how you go about doing your laundry is time well spent if you find time that you can use to do others things that you want to do in your life.

Assess

- Do you do your own laundry?
- Do you do laundry for other people?
- Do you use a laundromat or do you wash and dry your clothes at home?
- Do you wash and dry a load a day or do all your laundry on the same day?

- Do you do your laundry on the same day each week?
- Do you have any methods to remind you when a load of clothes is done and ready to turn over from washer to dryer?
- Do you fold your clothes on the same day you wash them?
- Do you have places to put your laundry after cleaning them?
- Do you share the washing machine and dryer with other people and do you need to schedule the time you do your laundry?
- Do you have laundry detergent and conditioning products on hand when you are ready to do the laundry?

Plan

Cheryl Mendelson has written a know-everything book about laundry called *Laundry: The Home Comforts Book of Caring for Clothes and Linens*.[23] In this book, Mendelson covers everything one needs to know about laundering cloth from reading the label and learning the fabric terms to sorting clothes, to removing stains, to laundering tricky items. Mendelson provides detailed information on how to launder everything from the kitchen rags to bedding, hand-washables, and baby clothes to vintage linens. She provides tips that are practical and an aid to anyone who does laundry – whether it is for the first load of clothes washed in a college dorm or for someone who has done hundreds of loads of laundry. The book would be a wonderful gift to share with anyone who does laundry.

<u>Goal - long range:</u>

- Reduce the time spent doing laundry

<u>Objective(s) - future condition(s):</u>

- To increase the number of times that all clothes for the family are washed on the same day once a week
- To decrease the number of times clothes wait in the washer to be moved to the dryer after each load

- To increase the number of times that clothes are folded immediately after taking them out of the dryer
- To decrease the total number of hours that it takes to complete the laundry process each week

Performance Indicator(s) - current condition(s):

- Number of hours spent in doing regular laundry by month

Do

No one is going to do a check sheet on the number of pieces of clothes washed and dried versus the number of hours that it takes to do the laundry. This thought brings at least a small smile from most people reading this book. Examining the amount of time required to do the process allows use of the quality improvement model. One area of focus is how the laundry collection and the process for getting the clothes ready for washing and drying. Some people know never to leave anything in their pockets because the person who does the wash never checks pockets. However, the person who does the laundry must check pockets for items like a red crayon, or a blue ink pen, or Chap Stick, or a phone, or a wallet. Changing this one habit will change the amount of time needed to do the laundry as the one who does the laundry will not have to get into stain removal and the person who left the item may not have to go get a new phone or driver's license.

Placing a check sheet in the laundry area allows data collection on the number of hours it takes for laundry process completion. See Figure 2 below. Record the number of hours it takes to accomplish the laundry each week and note strategies to decrease the time spent weekly. Be sure to put a pencil close by so that you can put in the information easily.

Date	Number of Hours to Do Laundry	Strategies to Decrease the Number of Hours Doing Laundry

Figure 2. Laundry Hour Check Sheet

Check

Look for the pattern where you can reduce the time it takes to do the laundry. I have been doing laundry for over 50 years for myself to 15 people at a time. I have my husband trained to take everything out of his pockets before he puts anything into the laundry. I admit this was harder to do when I had children in the house.

Recently, I learned that the order of doing the load of clothes helped speed the process for me. Now, I always wash the bed linen and remake the bed first. Then I move to the white load of towels and then to the dark jeans, and then to the dark load of knits, and finally to the white load of underwear. Have you given any thought to the order of washing clothes? I believe it has helped me get the clothes washed, dried and put away in about five hours once a week. Also starting the process at 6 AM will help to eliminate interruptions on washday.

Review

Managing the laundry scene will change with time as one goes from having a small baby in the house, to busy toddlers playing in the mud, to a teenage girl who changes her clothes several times a day, to caring for an elderly parent who has Alzheimer's Disease. Making adjustments in the process periodically will result in clean clothes ready to wear with the minimum amount of time spent on the process.

> **Time Management Outcome – Find Your Time by Reducing Time Spent Doing Laundry**
>
> Having clothes in the closet and drawers when you are ready to dress each day is worth spending time to plan a better method for doing the laundry. You soon will forget the times when you washed out the uniform blouse every day so that you had something to wear to school or work.

Taking Pictures of Possessions

Okay so you have been wondering how taking pictures of your possessions is going to find your time. Let me set the stage. Today it was really hot outside. The heat has hit 100 degrees for several days in a row. We were out in our car running errands and on the horizon, the black billows of smoke took over the clear skies. Ravaging fire overtook four houses within seconds from children playing with matches. It was over within minutes, the belongings of the inhabitants were all gone. There was nothing left except smoldering embers.

No one expects their houses to burn, no one expects the tornado to make matchsticks of their belongings, and no one expects the water to bring the thick, brown mud into their homes.

It is less dramatic but more common that one needs to find information about how something works months after purchase or to finding a part number to buy a replacement. Almost everyone has lost something – a camera on the fishing trip – or had someone take something from his or her home or car and needed to replace it. Have you ever lost your purse or wallet, or known someone who has? Do you remember what a nightmare it was?

Sandie Barrie

Therefore, deciding to get control over what it is you own and the filing of relevant paper brings comfort. Spending time now will save time later if you should need to be able to recall everything you own, or even just find the user manual for the item you purchased two months ago, or retrieve a picture of a stolen item.

Assess

- Do you know what you own?
- If you had to replace the contents of your home, do you know where you would start?
- Can you find the receipt for the item you bought last month that no longer functions?
- Do you want to be able to find information quickly when your spouse is trying to fix something by the "trial and error method" and he is getting more frustrated by the minute?

Plan

As you look around the room you are sitting in while reading this book, you can see many items. It is a bit overwhelming to think about putting everything you own into a database. One then needs to set up a system to capture new items when bringing them into the house and removing items when discarded. Besides itemizing belongings, it is also important to organize the relevant paperwork that is associated with the belongings, which can include the receipt, the user manual, and relevant part sheets. Do you have paper copies of the cards you carry in your purse or wallet? It's much easier to cancel and notify companies if you have this information stored separately in a safe place.

After some review, I found a program called My Stuff Deluxe to help me in the process. My Stuff Deluxe provides a low-cost solution for recording items into a database including relevant paperwork. Locate My Stuff Deluxe http://www.contactplus.com/products/freestuff/mystuff.htm. Using Microsoft Access 2003, one can build a similar database. Finding the program was the easy part, even figuring out how to use it was easy. Now the real fun starts in developing a plan that helps me actually get the task done. It seemed so overwhelming and I knew that the process itself was going to take time. Table 5 below provides a plan and timeline to record belongings.

Table 5 - Record Belongings Timeline

	Week 1	Week 2	Week 3	Week 4
Purchase software and learn how to use software	X			
Gather laptop and camera and be sure know how to use equipment	X			
Determine functions to use for my situation		X		
Complete taking pictures and enter data into My Stuff Deluxe - first room		X		
Complete second room		X		
Complete third room			X	
Complete fourth room			X	
Complete fifth room				X
Make copy and place in safety deposit box				X

Goal - long range:

- Make a list of everything in the Barrie family home within one month

Objective(s) - future condition(s):

- To take a picture of all items in the Barrie family home room by room within one month
- To enter the information into My Stuff Deluxe for all items in the Barrie family home room by room within one month
- To place a thumb drive with the My Stuff Deluxe files into the safety deposit box within one day after completion of the process

Performance Indicator(s) - current condition(s):

- Initial recording of all items in My Stuff Deluxe
- Update the My Stuff Deluxe by adding new items and discarding old items from the database monthly
- Copy of updated My Stuff Deluxe file kept in the safety deposit box monthly

Do

I was still overwhelmed, even after developing a plan. I delayed the process for months because I kept telling myself that I did not want to put items into the database if I was going to get rid of them. Perfectionism was the culprit. I wanted everything to be perfect, so I just had to get over with the thought that I had to do this perfectly, and just start to take pictures in the sewing room so that I could get moving on the project. I found one time saver was to take a picture of the area on equipment where the serial and model numbers were located. It was not only easy, it was quick, and reduced the possibility that I would input the wrong data.

Check

As I moved through a room, took a picture, and put it in the database I could see that the database was growing. I soon realized that after all the information was collected at this one point in time, that the database would become outdated if I did not take the time once a month to say to myself, "Have I bought anything new or have I given or thrown something away that I had previously placed in the database?" Putting a recurring reminder in my Microsoft Outlook 2003 calendar to spend 30 minutes a week on this task helped me know that I would always have a current listing of my belongings.

Review

The last step is to make sure there are a couple of copies of the database output located outside of our home. Place the data on a computer disk or thumb drive and put it in a safety deposit box. If you live in tornado-prone area, you may also want to send a copy to a relative in another location or investigate into a cyberspace solution like Google Docs.

> **Time Management Outcome – Finding Your Time by Taking Pictures of Possessions**
>
> If you have ever lived through a flood, a tornado, or a fire, you understand the savings of time by having a record of your belongings to be able to take with you when you talk with your insurance adjuster. However, for most of us, we will find our time in not having to spend a lot of time to find a receipt or a user manual to some piece of equipment. Put time in the bank by making and storing important records.

In summary, see Appendix A for a table that demonstrates how one can monitor performance indicators by month for the household maintenance dimension. While you can use Microsoft Word 2003 or Microsoft Excel 2003 to develop this form, paper and pencil will accomplish the same goal of recording information on a monthly basis. Appendix B provides additional suggestions for situations for the household dimension where you can explore using the quality improvement model to make changes you desire in your life. The Selected Resources Section provides reference materials to help you as you develop your plan. Now that we have put some order to our household maintenance, let's move onto travel.

Sandie Barrie

Travel

I generally travel by car. However, I do remember when I was young that I did take a bus to school. Because we went to Catholic schools, the bus did not take us to our school but instead left us off at a corner about a mile from school where the bus turned to go to the public schools. I have taken an occasional bus and train trip in my adult life and three or four times a year I get on an airplane to travel to a conference or to see family. In addition, I do get on the back of my husband's motorcycle to enjoy a ride on a warm summer day. However, for me, traveling by car has been my main means to get from one place to another. Some people have to get into a car every day while others can choose to take public transportation and have never driven a car. Nevertheless, we all know that time is saved by taking modern transportation to travel to the places we desire to go. Using the quality improvement model, three situations are studied in the travel dimension: planning where you are going, maintaining your vehicles, and reducing travel annoyances.

Planning Trips

I needed to go southbound on I-395 from Sparks to the south side of Reno for a meeting. I had even been to the location many times before, but my mind was foggy. I kept asking myself, *Do I get off on Plumb or Moana?* I knew if I made the wrong choice, I was going to be late for the meeting and I so wanted to appear professional and be on time. I turned on

Moana Lane and crossed over Virginia Street when I realized that things did not look right. I was going to be late because I had taken the wrong turn.

Assess

- When was the last time you got lost when you thought you knew where you were going?
- When you are planning to go to a destination that you are not familiar with, how do you determine how to get there?
- Do you take your own car or public transportation to get around from one place to another?
- What aids do you use when you are planning a trip?

Plan

I am married to a pilot who has an innate sense of being able to find his way around whether he is in an airplane, boat, motorcycle, or car. When we moved to the Reno-Sparks community 30 years ago, he pointed out that Mount Rose was to the southwest, Peavine was to the northwest, and that the then-named MGM Grand was to the east of Reno. With those kinds of landmarks, I have been able to get around in our town. However, take me out of familiar territory and I become turned around faster than a washing machine on high gear. Now that I am pursuing a writing career and have left the corporate life, I can travel outside of my local community. I find myself traveling alone without the assistance of my husband's innate senses, so I have had to learn how to use tools like MapQuest, GPS, and Google Earth.

Goal - long range:

- Develop a strategy to be able to find a location when I am traveling

Objective(s) - future condition(s):

- Plan in advance for short trips

Sandie Barrie

- Plan in advance for long trips

Performance Indicator(s) - current condition(s):

- Number of times where I got lost on a short trip per month
- Number of time times when I got lost on a long trip per month

Do

I love maps, and I even understand them when I look at them – the years of being married to my pilot husband have helped. One trick he taught me is to turn the map in the right direction. In other words, orient the map to the north direction. My husband uses maps almost exclusively. I, on the other hand, have been a user of MapQuest for years. The turn-by-turn directions are very helpful. There are a few minor problems since MapQuest does not identify construction work and does not provide directions for the detours. The problem I have is that I wear glasses to read and I do not need the glasses when I am driving. Therefore, I almost have to stop the car to see what I need to do next. Some of you know exactly what I am describing. I was glad when MapQuest made the font on the directions larger – that helped, but I still feel challenged when I am trying to drive and read MapQuest directions, especially at night.

Buying the GPS was the easy part. I still remember how I thought I could just go out and use it without spending much time to learn its functions, and try to drive at the same time. Therefore, I decided that I needed to take some time when I was not driving to figure the program out. It really was not that difficult. There is no check sheet here. You will know immediately if you are on track or not as the voice from the GPS screeches out in a fatiguing tone, "re-cal-cu-la-ting" when you make a mistake.

Check

At first, I only learned the very basic elements of the program like how to find a specific address. As I learned and used the program more, I found places to eat and even shopping malls. I did find that there were limitations when I was looking for sewing stores, so when I am traveling in a strange area and want to find specialty stores I have learned that I need to do my research in advance so that I have a specific address to be able to program into the GPS.

Review

Once you have a GPS and you know how to use it, you will wonder why you waited so long to save your money to purchase one. It is also important to realize that printing out the maps using http://www.mapquest.com/ in advance gives you a back up, if for any reason, the GPS should malfunction.

> **Time Management Outcome – Find Your Time by Planning Trips**
>
> Being on time for a planned event is a worthy goal one I strive to accomplish. Having a GPS helps me arrive on time because I have not lost my way and being on time for valuable events helps me obtain the goals and objectives that are of interest to me.

Maintaining Vehicles

Having seven brothers made it easy in the early years, since the boys in our family did the outside things like maintaining vehicles. For the three years I was in nurses training, I lived in the dorm and walked to those places like the local restaurant that I wanted to go. I really did not drive much until I got married and I still never worried about maintaining vehicles since my husband had been a farm boy and all this stuff about keeping vehicles running, like oil changes, changing batteries, and fixing flat tires was second nature to him.

For the first 10 years of our marriage, you could go to the local gas station and the men who worked there pumped the gas, cleaned the windows, and checked the battery and oil. I just sat in the car, made sure I was pleasant, and thanked the men as I drove away. Even in the last 20 years or so since I have learned how to pump my own gas, I still have a local tire store where I can go to get my tires checked/changed or to get a battery replaced. In addition, I go to one of the local oil changing places every three months and have them check the vehicle over and change the oil. It seems easy.

I have never kept track of maintenance on my vehicle. If the car turns over when I turn the key over, I consider myself good to go. Then one day in the late summer, my car did not start. Of course, I called my husband and he asked me several questions and told me to call AAA to have them tow it to the dealership.

What happened next took about eight months to resolve. To make a long story short, my car didn't start at my home on August 11th, AAA came and tried to start the car, and then when it didn't start, hauled it to the dealership. I had AAA service so there was no charge. The dealer replaced the starter and I paid $572.38 two days later. My husband had a new battery installed on September 5th. All went well until September 8th, when again in my garage, the car would not start. A different tow service truck came since the dealership determined that I had coverage for this and when they got the car to the dealership, the car started, they drove it around for a few days and it did not fail. I got it back. On September 22nd, I could not start the car. This time the dealer replaced the cooling fan and the starter. The mechanic drove the car around and it started each time. The car was returned on September 30th and I paid a $100 deductible.

Assess

- Do you change your own oil?
- Do you have someone regularly service your car?
- Do you know what your tire pressure should be? Do you check your tire pressure periodically?
- Do you keep track of the maintenance done on all your vehicles?

Plan

Goal - long range:

- Demonstrate what maintenance has been done on each vehicle

Objective(s) - future condition(s):

- To log ongoing tire and battery changes done on PT Cruiser
- To log ongoing oil changes done on PT Cruiser
- To log ongoing other maintenance done on PT Cruiser

Performance Indicator(s) - current condition(s):

- Maintenance log completed on PT Cruiser by month

Do

Okay, so it was time for action. I decided to use Microsoft Excel 2003 to establish a log for the maintenance of my vehicles. I started with the PT Cruiser since it had been giving me the most problems over the last eight months. First, I called the dealership to obtain copies of the maintenance records for my vehicle. Then, I called the place where I had the car's oil changed and asked about getting a log of oil changes. Lastly, I called my tire place and, as usual, they were very helpful and said that I could stop by and pick up the log that they could print off their computer program. After getting the papers together, I entered a few elements to include: the date of service, the maintenance activity, and the mileage. A simple log provided a timeline for what had occurred over the last 8 months on my PT Cruiser (see Figure 3 below).

Date	Maintenance Activity	Mileage
8/13/2008	Replaced starter	59330
9/3/2008	Tire rotation and balance	59594
9/5/2008	Battery replaced	
9/30/2008	Replaced starter	59900
10/28/2008	Oil changed	
11/20/2008	Would not start, but no problem found	61399
12/8/2008	Repaired flat	
1/20/2009	Replaced switch	61901
1/20/2009	Replaced wiring harness, engine compartment	61901
1/21/2009	Air filter replaced	
1/29/2009	Starter hit with long rod and starts and starter replaced	61981
4/3/2009	Oil changed	62552
4/20/2009	Would not start, starter hit with long rod and starts and solenoid found defective and replaced	62760

Figure 3. Partial maintenance log for PT Cruiser

Check

Therefore, here's the analysis. In eight months and in driving 3,430 miles, my PT Cruiser has had three new starters and the last starter had a defective solenoid. I don't know about you, but to say that I was ready to sell this car is an understatement. I have not made this up for the purposes of this book; this is a real story. In the process, I also realized that the very first starter that was put in was under warranty and that I should not have paid the $500-plus for it. That mistake cost me time in figuring out how to get my money back and writing letters to complete paperwork in order to get my money back. So now, I have added to my maintenance log the start and end dates of the maintenance agreements.

Review

Now that I have the PT Cruiser done, I need to do the same thing for the other vehicles that my husband and I own and then I can put into my calendar when I might expect to need to change the oil in the short-term and the battery and tires in the long-term for all my vehicles.

Let's hope after three starters and one part for the last starter that we don't have to replace that again.

> **Time Management Outcome – Find Your Time by Maintaining Your Vehicles**
>
> Think about the last time that your car didn't start. At best, it is an inconvenience, but if the inconvenience happened because you did not take time to change the oil, check the tire pressure, or to take the car in to find out why there is a noise every time you step on the brakes, then you need to expect an interruption will occur to your schedule. Finding time to maintain vehicles will save time in the end because you can schedule needed actions on your time.

Reducing Travel Annoyances

In February of this year I made two trips – one to Palm Desert, Calif., and one to Puyallup, Wash. I packed a bag for both trips. For the first trip, I had the luxury of traveling in my own vehicle, while on the second trip, I went by plane. On the first trip, I was gone for six days, and on the second trip, I was gone for five days. Packing for the second trip was much more difficult because I had to condense everything to two bags. For both trips, I packed the day before I traveled and so for both trips, I had to rethink what it was that I wanted to take. I expect that I will be making more trips now that I am retired, which is different from what I have done in previous years when I was either working at a job or working at renovating our home.

Traveling in modern society is common. Some of our trips are done once or twice a year when we go back to visit relatives if we live away from our home of origin. There are many variables to traveling depending on how and where we travel. Some people make frequent trips or always have a bag packed since they do not know when their work will require that they be away from their home. There are many restrictions to what one can include in a suitcase when it comes to traveling by air. The traveler wants to include needed items to have when they get to their destination. You do not want to get to the side of your son's hospital bed in a city a couple thousand miles away without your dentures or your medicines.

Assess

- How many times do you travel in a year that requires you to pack a bag or two?
- If you need to make a trip in a hurry because of an impending fire, flood, or other weather event, are you able to find all the things that you need and pack the bag in an hour or less?
- Do you have a list of those things that you want to be sure you have with you to keep you comfortable or to meet your medical or work needs?
- Do you have a method to replace those articles that you have used from your travel bag before you stow your bag?

Plan

Looking at your particular situation and having a good idea of how much you travel and what your needs are will drive the degree of preparation needed.

<u>Goal - long range:</u>

- To be ready to pack a bag to travel within one hour

<u>Objective(s) - future condition(s):</u>

- To have a list of items needed to pack a bag to travel
- To identify essential versus non-essential items needed to travel
- To identify those items that need to be replaced prior to stowing bags between trips

Performance Indicator(s) - current condition(s):

- Reviewed list prior to travel and after travel to determine if any additions or deletions need to be made

Do

Okay, I don't have a travel list and I am getting ready to travel on May 6th, so I decided today to make one for myself. I started by making a list of items needed to pack a bag to travel. Well to start it was easy for me: tea bags, debit card, and medications and I could go anywhere. Then I sat down with pen and paper and put together the serious list of the rest of the items I needed to take with me. See Table 6 for a general packing list for women. Be sure to slip a copy of the check sheet into the bag before finally closing it up.

Table 6 – General Packing List for Women

	Under clothes
	Outer clothes
	Medications
	Hygiene Items
	Electrical Equipment (batteries, chargers)
	Sleeping Needs
	Shoes
	Money (charge or debit cards)
	Insurance Card
	Maps
	Address List

Check

The check sheet developed as one packs can serve to assist the traveler in backing their suitcase when they are ready to come home. Remember to place a copy in the suitcase before you finally close it.

Review

Once you are back home, you can review the check sheet and determine if there is anything else you would include on the list, as well as, replenish any supplies so that the bag is ready for the next trip.

> **Time Management Outcome – Find Your Time by Reducing Travel Annoyances**
>
> You will not have to go back to the front desk on arrival to ask if they have any toothpaste or a toothbrush. You will not have to go to the local pharmacy to pick up medication or other toiletries that you require for your general comfort or survival. You will be more comfortable as you try to entertain a young child or a fragile elderly parent as you wait out an unexpected weather event in a strange environment.

In summary, see Appendix A for suggested performance indicators for travel. While you can use Microsoft Word 2003 or Microsoft Excel 2003 to develop this form, paper and pencil will accomplish the same goal of recording information on a monthly basis. Appendix B provides additional suggestions for aspects of the travel dimension, where you can explore using the quality improvement model to make changes you desire in your life. The Selected Resources Section provides reference materials to help you as you develop your plan. Now that we have evaluated and put in place better systems for our travel, let's evaluate our finances dimension.

Finances

Receipts are the little pieces of paper we receive when we purchase items. Receipts reflect what we spend on the expense side of our operating budgets. I have not always paid attention to the little piece of paper called a receipt. I do place it in a file folder so that I could find it if I wanted to return an item or to have it in case I wanted to itemize my sales tax for a given year for my IRS return.

I purchased some fabric at a local fabric store. I have the usual fabric stash that most longtime seamstresses have so I looked at the 30% off and the price at $11.99 and figured out that four yards of the fabric should cost me about $8.00 per yard or $32. I also purchased some small rolls of fabric and the sign said $.88, which was regularly $1.29.

When I got ready to do the purchase, I swiped my debit card, punched in my PIN (personal identification number), and waited for the card reader to tell me my purchase was approved, all the time chatting with the clerk about the weather. The clerk handed me the receipt and I went out the door. When I got home and went to file the receipt, I looked at it more closely and determined that the stock keeping unit, or SKU number, had the fabric at $13.99 instead of $11.99. Additionally, the computer did not recognize the SKU number for the $1.29 item and therefore did not show the correct price of $.88. Eventually, I determined I had a return coming equaling more than $15 (which buys several gallons of gasoline).

The above examples demonstrate how easy it is for money to escape from our pockets and can damage our intention to manage our money. Using the quality improvement model, three situations are inspected in the finances dimension: reducing fear in developing an operating budget, saving money, and taking control of investments.

Reducing Fear in Developing an Operating Budget

Years ago, I started to use a budget for my revenue and expenses. I really don't know where I learned this or why I started the process, but it is not that difficult to do. You can start by asking a few questions.

Assess

- How much time do you spend on your personal financial budget?
- How many years have you maintained a budget?
- What are the two largest sources of revenue?
- What are the five largest expenses in your budget?
- What do you do with your receipts?
- When was the last time you went through your budget to see if there were line items where you could save on without changing your lifestyle?
- Have you given any thought to changing your perspective on how you manage your money?

Plan

Initially, I read a book by David Bach called *Smart Women Finish Rich*[24] that was the catalyst for me to examine my financial affairs. Over the last six months, Suze Orman has been on television promoting her book, *Suze Orman's 2009 Action Plan: Keeping Your Money Safe and*

Sound.[25] I learned about this book one day when I was listening to Oprah and Orman was making a presentation. At the end of the show, Oprah offered the book free as a downloadable document. I downloaded the document immediately to my computer. Thanks, Oprah! Then I methodically read the book and determined where I was doing things correctly and where I needed to make improvements. One area that I spent some time on was the operating budget for the Barrie household.

Goal - long range:

- Maintain an ongoing operating budget for the Barrie household

Objective(s) - future condition(s):

- To determine all income sources on a monthly basis
- To determine all outgoing expenses on a monthly basis

Performance Indicator(s) - current condition(s):

- Determine checking account balance monthly
- No credit card purchases per month

Do

Develop a budget by simply listing all your income sources and then all your outgoing expenses. See Suze Orman's website, where she has placed a work sheet that identifies many of the standard budget items at http://www.suzeorman.com. Take the time to calculate whether the expense goes out one time or if it is a recurring expense that happens monthly or at the same time each year. There is nothing like forgetting that the Department of Motor Vehicles' annual registration is due next week when you already have spent your extra money on the fancy sports shoes for your son. Once you have a functioning budget that you regularly review, surprises are less likely. If you have checking accounts with online payment options, use them to handle your regular monthly payments. By setting up your recurring payments on a schedule, you will never have a late payment, which will help improve your Fair Isaac Company (FICO) score. It is worth the small fee required in some cases to ensure that your payments are always on time.

Check

After you put the budget together, be sure to look at it at least once a month, no matter how busy you are. When you look at your budget, keep an eye open for what has changed in your life, what may have changed in society, what new revenue sources are available, and what new expenses are coming or may be coming that may require that you adjust your budget.

Review

Once a year, take a really hard look at all your revenues and expenses and project what you expect to have coming in and going out for the next year. The more time you spend identifying elements of your operating budget, the more money you will have for needed and desired capital budget items like houses, cars, boats, or home renovations. More importantly, you will be more in control over how your money is spent and you will have reserves set aside for times when you need extra money.

> **Time Management Outcome – Find Your Time by Reducing Fear in Developing An Operating Budget**
>
> Each year that you develop your budget enables you to be more and more in control of your fears that you will not have enough money to meet some perceived need. You will be able to stop using credit cards and be able to pay off your last one. Then you can work on your last outstanding debt – the mortgage – knowing that you are taking steps every day to pay it off helps reduce the fear inside of you that you will lose your home to foreclosure as you age. This is time well spent!

Saving Money

Even when you have budgeting down and you plan it all out, you will find that something will come up that you need extra money. It doesn't even have to be as dramatic as losing a job. It could be the starter on your car that needs repair, or a flat tire on your motorcycle, or needing three crowns in the same month. If you have put money aside, then you can simply use it to deal with the situation at hand.

Therefore, even though I have had and maintained a budget for years, I still have two problems. The first problem is that I have never really examined my budget for potential savings and secondly, I have never really done a good job at putting even $10 a month away on a regular basis because there was no line item in my budget for savings.

Therefore, when the above situations came up, I had to find the money out of my current operating budget, which messed things up and was discouraging to the whole process.

Sandie Barrie

Assess

- How much time do you spend on your savings program?
- Are you able to put away $10 per month and leave it in the savings account?
- Do you check your receipts for errors?
- Do you return items that do not meet your expectations?

Plan

My plan was very simple. I grabbed an old vase and put it on my desk and started to put some coins into it that I saved by making better choices while I was spending money. Living on a budget is not that difficult to do. However, you need to pay attention to potential savings in many areas. Take time to examine whether you can take a generic medication for your brand medication. Check into options for your car insurances. Check the accuracy of receipts. Take the time to look for a sale when purchasing needed items. Return items that don't meet your expectations. Stop charges when you do not get expected services. Purchase books online. Use coupons at your regular places for shopping such as car maintenance or your favorite dining establishment.

In just six weeks, I found the following opportunities to find my money and it really did not take me much time to save hundreds of dollars. I found that if my husband and I changed the statin medication that we used, we could save $80 per month. We changed the type of insurance on one of our vehicles, saving us $30 per month. I complained about a damaged piece of furniture shipped to me (small but noticeable scratch) and got $95 off my purchase. I ordered a national newspaper and when it did not arrive for three weeks over the holiday, I decided I really didn't need that newspaper and I cancelled the subscription saving me $15 per month. At my favorite bookstore, I found four small books at 70% off saving me $8.32 and put them on my gift shelf for that last minute, I-need-something-to-bring-to-this-party-as-I-am-walking-out-the-door nights (saving me time from going to the store to purchase something). I saved $10 on an air cleaner for my car by using a coupon that I got at my last oil change. I saved $9.05 by purchasing three books on http://www.Amazon.com and having them shipped to my home and I saved time by not driving to my local bookstore and searching the shelves to see if they had copies available. I saved $6 at my local pizza place by using a coupon that I had gotten the month before. I found that I could save $25 per month in service fees by simply transferring $150 from my checking to my savings account monthly and they don't charge me if I have to transfer it back. I made a blouse for my granddaughter for her birthday from my fabric stash and saved $15. I found an option to be able to get free continuing education hours for my professional license, which will save me an estimated $300 this year. In addition, just today as I was really looking at my receipts that I was reviewing in preparation of my taxes, I found overcharges of $500 on car maintenance work done earlier in the year.

Now that I have whetted your appetite for finding some money, and as you are doing your research to develop your own personal plan, you might want to look at *Suze Orman's 2009 Action Plan: Keeping Your Money Safe and Sound* where you can find a chapter dedicated to spending.

Goal - long range:

- To have a stash of cash to cover eight months of operating expenses for the Barrie budget

Objective(s) - future condition(s):

- To evaluate opportunities to find savings with purchases that are made on a regular basis
- To evaluate opportunities to use coupons to reduce the cost of purchases made on a regular basis
- To evaluate whether reductions to the expected budgeted items can be made during the year
- To ensure that no new credit card charges are made during the year

Sandie Barrie

Performance Indicator(s) - current condition(s):

- Number of dollars in savings account recorded on last day of month
- Number of new credit card charges recorded on last day of month

Do

I started a little game with myself where when I use a coupon, find an error in a receipt, purchase books online, save costs on medications, reduce car insurance costs, make a gift instead of buying one, I place the saved money in the old vase on my desk. It is fun to watch the money build up from a dollar saved here and a dollar saved there.

Check

Initially, I just jotted the few cents here and the few cents there that I was saving on a Post-it note. It did not take long for the dollars to start adding up. Of course, when it gets to be more than a few dollars, be sure to put it in a safe place – it would be a shame to see the savings go up in a fire or blow away in a tornado. It will be fun at Christmastime to look at the savings account and determine what I can do with that money. By then, perhaps I will have enough cash in the savings account to have the eight-month stash of money that Orman suggests that we all have in reserves. It will be fun to see how close I am to that goal.

Review

Well I have been on my new game for three months and I have found a total of $1,287.00 so I will be continuing this effort. I can hardly wait until December 31, 2009 to see what my final total is. I just want to share this strategy with everyone.

> **Time Management Outcome – Find Your Time by Saving Money**
>
> Finding money to put into a savings account is just pure joy knowing that you will have money to pay for something when an unexpected expense arrives. You will save time by not having to worry about how to cover the expense; or arguing with your spouse over the problem; or going out and finding a second job to cover the expense.

Taking Control of Investments

I am not an expert on investments. I did not learn how to invest money at a young age. Neither my family nor schoolteachers taught investment strategies to me. A portion of the small allowance I was given by my dad for working in the floral shop was used by my mom to pay the milk bill. The concept of investing some of my money for my retirement never entered my head as a young person. After all, we lived from one paycheck to the next. I was probably in my 40s when I first realized that I could save some money on my taxes if I put some money in an individual retirement account (IRA).

It was a start, but I never managed that money very well. I didn't understand the statements when they came. I never even opened them. The information about the stock market was too dense for me to understand, and besides, there were all the excuses about not having enough time. Eventually I tried to learn more about it, but I was nervous about taking chances with money and the topic of investment did not excite me! Now, at age 63, I wish I had been wiser about investments as I calculate how much money that I will need to sustain my husband and myself, as we get ready for retirement.

Assess
- How much time do you spend on your investments?
- Do you have someone who manages your money?

- Do you open the investment envelopes that come in the mail?
- Do you get statements and related investment materials online or sent to you by e-mail?

Plan

About two years ago, I read a book titled, *Smart Women Finish Rich* by David Bach.[26] At the time, I was starting to think about retirement. I wanted to stop working at the day job. I read the book cover to cover. I was still overwhelmed. I learned from the book that there were many things that I did not understand and so, in that respect, the book was very helpful. The brokerage firm changed the individual who was handling my account. The broker who had my account was not in my town and I decided I wanted someone I could speak with one-on-one, face-to-face on a regular basis. I can still remember the day I went and spoke to the man. He asked many questions. I was not only overwhelmed; I felt the broker was only after my money and not interested in teaching me what to do. He just didn't seem to have time to listen and answer *my* questions. One day, he called, and I answered the phone while I was driving and he wanted to do business, even after I told him I could not talk at that time. I decided to change brokerage firms. The new brokerage firm came to me from a recommendation from my husband's employer. In addition, with it, came a woman who was willing to learn about my situation and me and to help me understand what I needed to do to invest properly and to manage the investments that I had.

Goal - long range:

- To monitor retirement investments

Objective(s) - future condition(s):

- To review the value of investment accounts monthly
- To meet with investment counselor to review accounts quarterly
- To evaluate whether investments have grown in value from previous year annually

Performance Indicator(s) - current condition(s):

- Review investment statements monthly

Do

For me, I needed to find someone who was interested in helping me understand investments. I found a firm that had a systematic way to monitor investments. I now schedule a meeting with the new broker at least twice a year so that we can review what it is that is occurring with the markets. I maintain my investment file in my monthly call-up file so I have to look at it at least once a month.

Check

With the use of technology and the help of the administrative assistant of the broker, I can now go online and find one page that gives me the total dollar figure for my investments. Immediately, I can determine if my investments are increasing or decreasing. I now spend time on the monthly review, where for the most part, I am watching my money grow. The few times in the last couple of years when they have decreased, I have asked for a meeting with the broker to determine what is going on in the market and whether I needed to do anything. Finding the new broker was time well spent! She took the time to explain to me what was going on in the market.

Review

I was so pleased with the way I was treated by the new broker, who took the time to educate me and counsel me on what strategies I should be using to invest my money, that I made a recommendation to my son to make an appointment with her (which he did). The new broker is now assisting him as well.

> **Time Management Outcome – Find Your Time by Taking Control of Your Investments**
>
> It makes sense to learn early how to handle your investments by taking the time to meet with the person who is investing your money and to understand how your money is being invested. When you take the time to understand which papers to read and which ones to throw out you will not only save your time, you will be managing your time wisely when it comes to your investments.

In summary, see Appendix A for suggested performance indicators for finances. While you can use Microsoft Word 2003 or Microsoft Excel 2003 to develop this form, paper and pencil will accomplish the same goal of recording information on a monthly basis. Appendix B provides additional suggestions for aspects of the finances dimension where you can explore using the quality improvement model to make changes you desire in your life. The Selected Resources Section provides reference materials to help you as you develop your plan. Now that we have evaluated and put in place better systems for our finances, let's evaluate our work dimension.

Find Your Time: Assess, Plan, Do, Check, Review

Work

Okay so the word "work" has the connotation of being something difficult and something one *has* to do. However, for most of us, we have to do something in order to earn money to be able to buy the things that we need to have (not only want) to exist in modern society. I grew up working. From the time I was a small child, there were lots of other brothers and sisters in my environment and we all had to contribute to be able to survive. We hunted, planted gardens, and worked in our dad's floral business. As we each became adults, we chose to enter different fields in order to sustain our lives. One could easily say that I am the eldest of a bunch of "workaholics" and "overachievers." Using the quality improvement model, three situations in the work dimension are explored: ongoing preparation for changing your career, employing volunteerism in finding new work, and readying the resume.

Ongoing Preparation for Changing Your Career

I was barely 18 at the time. I remember the incident like it was yesterday! The package I was waiting for had arrived in the mail. I carried it carefully down the long winding road to my home. I was so excited – it was the information from the Patricia Stevens Fashion Design School. I loved to sew and thought this was going to be my career in life until my mom saw that I had spent money on the information. She made me send it back because I had spent $100 on information about the school (probably a substantial amount of money for 1964). So instead, I spent 40 years in a career that I adjusted to but that was not what I really wanted to do with my life. Over 45 years ago, there were not the opportunities for women that there are today. Most women who worked outside of the home did so as nurses or teachers.

When I was young, I just wanted out of my home environment. Being the oldest of 13 children born in 16 years did have its challenges. As soon as I learned that my mom was going to make me send the package back, I started trying to figure out what else I could do with my life. A nurse from St. Mary's Hospital School of Nursing came to St. Joseph Seminary (the all-girls school high school I attended) and talked about nursing. The next day, I started to look at how I could get into the school. I really don't remember how the application got into my hand, and I soon learned that I was not going to get any financial help from my dad – there were too many mouths to feed. However, I did learn about a state grant that paid girls to go to school if they would work one year for each year that they went to school in the local state mental health institute. The grant even paid a very small stipend each month. Therefore, off I went! Forty-five years later, nursing has always provided me with job opportunities. If I lost one job, I could find another job easily. Even today, I know that if I have to find a job, I could get one somewhere. However, I am not sure that if I had it to do all over again and had the choices that women have now, I would have chosen nursing for my lifelong career (but that is another book).

Assess

- Regardless of what stage you are in life, are you doing what you really want to do with your work life?
- Are you doing something now that will contribute to what you really want to do and have an aptitude for doing the rest of your life?
- Are you stuck in a career that no longer interests you?
- Have you taken the time to undergo any testing to determine your aptitudes are?
- Have you decided to stay in a career because the money is too good and you just don't want to go through the psychological work to start over?
- Are you afraid of what others will say if you stop doing what you have always been doing because it no longer suits your health, your abilities, or your aptitude?

- Did you lose your job because computers or other changes in technology or the economy forced changes in your field of expertise?
- Do you want to get into your later years saying to yourself, *If I had only done that…?*
- What is the work that you really want to do?
- What work contributes to your life energy?

Plan

So how do you go about determining how you will spend your time while you earn a living or work? This is difficult to figure out since none of us has a crystal ball. We cannot see all the variables that will impact on this decision. No matter what age you are now, you may need or want to re-evaluate what you plan to do with the rest of your work life. When I was growing up, there were not many personality tests available for me to take. Personality or aptitude tests are generally a paper and pencil test. Now there are a variety of tests that can help you understand how your personality would mesh with certain career choices. One of my favorites is the Myers-Briggs Type Indicator. You can learn about this personality test by examining the work of Paul D. Tieger and Barbara Barron-Tieger. In their book, *Do What You Are: Discover the Perfect Career for You Through the Secrets of Personality Type – Revised and Updated Edition Featuring E-Careers for the 21st Century*.[27] Check out this website http://www.personalitytype.com/career_quiz . Another great resource in accomplishing what work is right for you has an interesting name and is a classic having been published for more than 30 years, *What Color Is Your Parachute? 2009: A Practical Manual for Job-Hunters and Career-Changers* by Dick Bolles.[28] The book has short exercises that help you understand what your skills are, how to get unstuck, and how to choose a career coach or counselor. In addition, if you are near retirement or retired, you might want to pick up a copy of Bolles book titled, *What Color Is Your Parachute? for Retirement: Planning Now for the Life You Want*.[29]

<u>Goal - long range:</u>

- Determine what I enjoy that contributes to my economic needs to help support my life energy

Objective(s) - future condition(s):

- To evaluate what my natural aptitudes are at this stage of life
- To examine my options and determine what type of work brings joy to my being
- To identify what abilities I want to use in order to make money to sustain daily economic needs
- To determine the physical/mental stamina needed to do the work

Performance Indicator(s) - current condition(s):

- Personal satisfaction with work completed by month
- Review ability to be able to meet economic needs, including reducing debt and finding money to accomplish play goals by month

Do

You might want to go directly to the chapter on finding your life mission and the "pink pages" where Bolles provides forms for skill identification or go to http://www.jobhuntersbible.com/. Bolles teaches us to evaluate our individual aptitudes with different work environments. What skill sets do you have? How does one search the Internet for job opportunities? It takes time to do the exercises and to use the Internet. You might even get a group of people together and do the searches and the exercises together. Take the time to make a check sheet of the chapter headings of Bolles' book. This will help see the progress you are making when you use one-week dates of completion to help you get through the valuable material presented in the book. Be sure to post the check sheet on your computer screen, bathroom mirror, or car dashboard to remind you that you are in the process of completing the exercises. Even if you are not looking for a job today and don't think you need to do the exercises you might find in doing the exercises you learn something about yourself that will help you to consider what you want to do in your retirement.

Check

Share the fact that you are reading Bolles' book with your family and ask them to read it with you. Take the time to create a small group around you that is reading the book and take an hour once a week to discuss what you have learned. If you know several people who are now out of work, get them together and develop a support group that discusses what you are learning and what you have tried. Discuss what is working and what is not working. Have one person be the leader to schedule meetings and make sure you are all consistently working together until everyone in your group has found work. Being on a job search by yourself is non-productive – get some energy going by getting people to help you do what it is that you need to do.

Review

Bolles' book has changed as the times have changed so it is worth putting in your Microsoft Calendar that you need to check in 2010 and every year after to see what Dick Bolles has to say about the job market and what one can do when they decide to retire (see Selected Resources). Even more fun is to write a short paragraph in a journal on the first day of each month whether your work is meeting your economic needs and whether you are obtaining happiness in the pursuit of your work. Then when you are my age, you can look back at these paragraphs and perhaps chuckle as you see how you learned to survive during changing times.

> **Time Management Outcome – Find Your Time by Ongoing Preparation for Changing Your Career**
>
> Realizing that every few years you need to look at what is going on in the world and job markets, what your skills are, and what it is you need to do to prepare yourself for your next pile of things to do will save you time. Tomorrow you could face the dilemma of learning that the job you had this morning is no longer going to be the job you will have tomorrow. At some point in your live, you should be able to merge what gives you energy with what you need for economic survival, as well as, to be able to maintain your needs in good times and bad times.

Employing Volunteerism in Finding New Work

Being the oldest of 13 children, I have had the opportunity to watch a lot of family members and their significant others look and find a variety of jobs. Some, like me, have had many different jobs along the same path, and they called it a career, mine being nursing. Many family members have had many jobs not related to one career. Wikipedia provides some thoughts on the terms career, work, and job. Wikipedia explains that the term "career" pertains to remunerative work and sometimes to formal education. A career is a course of successive situations that make up a person's occupation.[30]

Wikipedia explains that the word "work" as "an action or something you get paid for."[31] Wikipedia explains that the word "job" dates back to the industrial revolution. The term job conceived "a pile of things to do."[32] The word "job" often refers to work. The explanation for the word "job" struck me because it puts into perspective what a lot of people think about the work they do that brings in the money to buy their food and other essentials in life. Nevertheless, jobs provide great opportunities to try out different piles of things to do. You can determine what piles interest you more and how the piles of things make you feel, what kind of money you get for doing different piles of things, and what affects the job has on your body and your time.

Assess

- Do you think of your work as doing a pile of things?
- Is this your first pile of things that you have picked up, cleaned up, or put away?
- How many different piles of things or jobs have you had during your work life?
- Have you taken time to explore or test out different jobs that fall into the category of work that you think may interest you?
- Have you had many jobs that have no connections? Do your jobs all relate to one main theme (called a career) like nursing or engineering?
- Do you wish you had tried doing more piles of things, or jobs, in your life?
- What job would you do now if you had everything that you needed to be able to do the job?

Plan

So what is holding you back? Let's set out to develop a plan to get the job that you want now. First, we are not going to deal with all the fears or excuses about why you cannot get the job. Yes, you need to be realistic. I doubt my farmer brother-in-law wants to become a brain surgeon or that my pilot husband wants to work in a nursing home. However, I know that if I had the resources that are available now I probably would not have gone into nursing. The real question is not what is the job that you want but how do you get the job you want? In addition, what do you need to do to get the job you want?

Ah, the answer is not easy and I don't have a magic wand to answer that question for everyone who is reading this book who might want a quick fix for their current situation. However, I have had a few conversations with my daughter-in-law over the last six months and she has taught me a thing or two that I am willing to share. Here it goes.

Sandie Barrie

It doesn't matter whether you have a job now or not – if you want to do something different but you can't find a paying job, one thing that you could do is get involved in what you want to do by volunteering.

Goal - long range:

- Find volunteer opportunities that bring satisfaction to my life and expose me to new opportunities

Objective(s) - future condition(s):

- To review volunteer matching websites (see Selected Resources)
- To select three volunteer opportunities to evaluate
- To choose one new volunteer opportunity to make a contribution

Performance Indicator(s) - current condition(s):

- Number of volunteer opportunities examined by month
- Number of volunteer hours completed by month

Do

With the blessing of the Internet, it is easy to find volunteer opportunities in your neighborhood, especially if you live in a larger urban area. Just go to one of the websites where the opportunities are listed for nonprofit organizations that need help to fulfill their mission (see Selected Resources). Find something in the long list of opportunities that speaks to you! Do something different and make a difference!

When the job, or the pile of things that you are dealing with, no longer keeps you motivated or meet your needs, go out and find one thing – even if it's only for a couple hours a month – and share your talents. Remember, what goes around comes around, and with your new found skills and contacts, that job you have always wanted is potentially just around the corner.

Check

Be sure to check your resume today – have you acknowledged the volunteer work that you have done in your life? The interesting thing is that some of the volunteer software programs actually allow you to record the time you spend volunteering, letting you keep track of your efforts over time.

Review

When you volunteer as a way to find a job, change a job, or enhance a job, you will learn how to share this concept with your son who needs work, an elderly person who wants an activity to keep his sanity, or maybe someone who just has too much time on her hands. You will not only be offering them a solution for improvement, but you will be increasing your web of contacts that see you as someone who is willing to help.

Time Management Outcome – Find Your Time by Employing Volunteerism in Finding New Work

You can sit at home and brood about the fact that you don't have a job or you can go out and make opportunities for yourself. You can make opportunities for new jobs while you are still at a job. You just won't have as much time. Putting your best foot forward and volunteering some of your time and talent is one way to find opportunities when you don't think there are any possibilities. You will be surprised at how much volunteering helps keep your options open if your current pile of things goes away.

Readying the Resume

How many jobs have you had? How many jobs do you expect to have? The answer to the last question has changed dramatically over the last 50 years. My dad had the same job all his life – he owned and operated a floral shop. The floral shop started in 1870 and the tradition carried on today by my sisters. My brothers-in-law have had the same job for their entire lives. Since they were very young boys they have farmed a piece of property in Grant Park, IL. My husband, on the other hand, has been a farmer, a worker in a corn mill, a plant manager for a spice company, and a pilot, while I have had a dozen health care jobs. Dad never wrote a resume while every time I have applied for a job in my career. I have had to list all places of employment over many years in all the places I have worked. While Bolles indicated, in his book, *What Color Is Your Parachute? 2009: A Practical Manual for Job-Hunters and Career-Changers* that sending out resumes blindly will not likely bring success, it is important to have a resume when you get an interview since the interviewer will want to see it. What is your pattern of work? Are you just starting out or do you have a long work history?

Assess

- Do you have a current resume?
- When was the last time you updated your resume?
- Will your resume get you the next job you need to be able to survive or to advance in your career or enhance your life energy?

Plan

While my brothers-in-law will probably never write a resume, my sons and grandchildren will probably need to write and always maintain a resume in order to get their next jobs. While in years past, people stayed in the same job for most of their lives, now you find that the societal circumstances require that you always be on the outlook for where your next work will come from.

A resume is generally a simple piece of paper or two. Most job interviewers want to see a copy during the interview process. When a networking contact occurs, the person will often say, "Please send me your resume." Hundreds of books explain resume development. One book that is particularly well written and helpful is *Resume Magic: Trade Secrets of a Professional Resume Writer*.[33] Susan Britton Whitcom designed the book for people who are capable of carrying out a successful, self-directed job search. Susan Britton Whitcomb helps the reader go after the job they want using advertising strategies, choosing a flattering format, and teaching one how to write great copy. She uses tricks to make the resume reach out to potential employers.

Goal - long range:

- Maintain an ongoing resume

Objective(s) - future condition(s):

- To develop a current resume
- To review the current resume to determine if additions or deletions or consolidations are needed
- To adopt the current resume to match the requirements of the desired job or volunteer activity

Performance Indicator(s) - current condition(s):

- Resume reviewed and ready for applying for a job or volunteer opportunity monthly

Do

Go to http://www.amazon.com and buy a copy of *Resume Magic: Trade Secrets of a Professional Resume Writer* today even if you don't need to write or rewrite your resume. Unlike years before, where the piles of things to do never changed much, in today's world you don't know what the piles of things to do will look like in the future and how many times you will need to change your job. Having this book in your library is like having aspirin in the medicine cabinet when you get a headache. If tomorrow you find you need to rewrite your resume, you will be ready to start the task. In addition, to say the least, for most of us, finding a new job compares to getting rid of a headache – maybe even a migraine. Table 7 provides a list of major components for a basic resume.

Table 7 - Checklist for a Basic Resume

	Basic Contact Information
	Work Desired
	Education
	Work Experience
	Volunteer Experience

Check

Once every six months, taking out your resume and reviewing the content of the document helps you keep your resume current. Take the time now to make a date with yourself on your Microsoft Calendar to review your resume.

Review

So you found your last copy of your resume, you are retired, and you don't think you will ever need a job again. You might be wrong! You may simply need to find a new pile of things to do to keep your sanity! Having discovered your life's mission and identified your skills, looking at the job market, your current resume, and Britton's book you may determine you need to write a simple resume to get your next pile of things to do.

> ### Time Management Outcome – Find Your Time by Readying the Resume
>
> You never know what unforeseen changes can occur that require us to return to old work, or find new different work, or do some volunteer work. You are wise if you have a current resume ready for distribution. The difference of having a resume versus not having a resume ready may be the difference between handling the job loss with grace instead of depression.

In summary, see Appendix A for suggested performance indicators for work. While you can use Microsoft Word 2003 or Microsoft Excel 2003 to develop this form, paper and pencil will accomplish the same goal of recording information on a monthly basis. Appendix B provides additional suggestions for situations in the work dimension where you can explore using the quality improvement model to make changes you desire in your life. The Selected Resources Section provides reference materials to help you as you develop your plan. Now that we have evaluated and put in place better systems to ensure that we have work, let's evaluate the education dimension.

Education

Okay we got through kindergarten, then middle school, and high school. However, what did we do after that? How much thought did we give to what it was that we wanted to do with our time in school after our early years? When we were six, seven, or eight, we generally didn't get to decide if we would go to school or where it was we would spend our time. Our parents sent us to school. We just went. Later in life, we have more options. Using the quality improvement model three situations in the education dimension are examined: making good choices in deciding on college/technical work, going to classes, and completing assignments for classes. Forty-five years ago, there were many limitations on what a young girl could choose to do with her opportunity for education.

Sandie Barrie

Making Good Choices in Deciding on College/Technical Work

Sister Irene pulled me aside and asked me what I was going to do after I left St. Joseph Seminary, the all girls' Catholic high school. She knew that I was going to go into nursing. Nevertheless, I did not realize what she really was asking – whether I understood the consequences of going to a diploma nursing program. There was no credit given toward a college degree. Neither my mom nor my dad had gone to any college and I never knew what the consequences of a college degree, pro or con, meant. For me, the diploma without college credits has served me well! Even though I have earned many other college degrees in my life, none of them has been in nursing. My career was nursing. It is obvious that I did not go to school to get ahead in my career.

Assess

- What stage of life brings you to this page, are you graduating from high school, trying to determine if you want to go to college/technical school?
- Have you really given thought to what it is you want to do for a great portion of your life?
- Have you just lost your job and want to calculate where the next money is going to come from in this technological era?
- Have you retired from a career or job that has served you well and now want to learn new skills to prepare yourself for uncertain financial times?
- Do you have a thirst for learning and just can't stop finding out about something new and different?
- Do you want to learn more about your favorite hobby?
- Have you determined how you are going to pay for the educational pursuits you desire?

Plan

There are so many opportunities to search out information about different educational opportunities as you explore why you want to go back to school. You can start with the Internet and get an overview about different careers or jobs. You can look at what your friends are doing and going through as they pursue their goals. You can step into your dad's shoes as my sisters did with my dad's floral shop, established in 1870, and learn about their life's work at the hand of our dad. You can trip off to something that looks like fun to a farmer sitting on a tractor like my husband did as he made up his mind that he wanted to fly airplanes. It is beyond the scope of this book to assist you in determining why you are going back to school. Know that whatever you aspire to do in life you may want to choose to get some background information through what we commonly call "education." You can start today by defining your goal for your next educational pursuit and whether college/technical school will serve you best in doing what you are passionate about. Know that once you make a decision, you will save a lot of time in the process if you spend some time deciding where you will go to school and how you will go about learning what it is you are interested in doing. Based on the answers to the questions in the assess section, you can then move to defining your goals, objectives, and performance indicators. While many people aspire to go to college, many others will want to go to a technical school to learn the valuable life-long skills they want. Technical schools are for job specific training for specific labor, such as, culinary arts or office manager. The country as a whole needs more nurses – people who want to help others and where nursing feeds their life energy. While you may not want to become a nurse, the preparation process that follows can be adapted to what you want to do.

Goal - long range:

- Become a nurse within five years

Objective(s) - future condition(s):

- Determine if I have the personality, the health, the intelligence, and tolerance to become a nurse
- Take some skill personality tests to determine if my aptitude for work meets my perception of the type of nursing I will desire to do
- Research out the requirements to become a nurse in the state I desire to live
- Research out the places to study nursing in the state I desire to live

- Research out the schools of nursing available in the state where I desire to live
- Research out the requirements to attend the schools of nursing and whether the school has a waiting list to get in
- Compare my education preparation and determine if I have the prerequisite courses to enter the school of nursing
- Research out the communities where the schools of nursing are located and determine if I will be able to afford to live in the community while I attend school
- Spend some time in the setting (hospital, doctor's office, surgical suite, emergency room) that I desire to do nursing in when I am done
- Determine if I am willing to make the sacrifices needed to accomplish my goal and give some thought to what I will do if some life event gets in the way of accomplishing my goal
- Determine how much schooling is going to cost, including lodging, books, Internet access, and other needed supplies

Performance Indicators (current conditions):

- Complete educational preparation plan by one year from start of evaluation to include:
    - appropriateness of chosen field for me
    - availability of school to obtain education (college versus technical)
    - requirements for entry into school
    - appropriateness of community (live in city of origin or move to new environment)
    - budget for expenses to attend school

Do

The more research you can do about what it is you want to spend a significant time commitment to go into will help you to make your final decision. It is helpful to design your own check sheet to ensure that you have covered all the facets of the evaluation process and to assign some dates to accomplish these tasks. Table 8 provides a check sheet for making a decision on college or technical work. One of the most important things in pursuing such a long-term goal, such as becoming a nurse, is to realize that part of the preparation is to realize early that some unforeseen challenges will meet you as you move along your educational path.

Table 8 – Sample Check Sheet for Making a Decision on College or Technical Work

Date	Criteria	Notes
	Have physical and mental stamina to complete _____	
	Skill appraisal tests demonstrate ability to function in _____	
	Has completed volunteer hours in area of interest _____	
	Knows criteria to enter program including prerequisites and application process for _____	
	Find places in local community where programs are offered for _____ and interview school and current/past students about the program	
	Identify specific requirements for entering program for _____	
	Develop a budget for costs related to program for _____	
	Obtain funding to attend program for _____	

Check

Once one has all the research done and a firm plan in place to pursue a college degree or job-specific technical school, sharing the plan and the check sheet with a trusted relative, friend, or counselor will help you determine if you have covered all needed issues. Realize that it is important as you move forward with the implementation of your plan to check your decision periodically. You want to be sure that when you are done with your educational plan you will have invested your time wisely. If you learn something about yourself in the process that questions the path you have chosen, take the time to think about what is going on, talk it over with trusted individuals, and if necessary, correct or change your course.

Review

This is an easy section for me to write because I have many lessons learned on this topic. I will not spend time here talking about what I would do differently if I had it to do all over, since, as I said earlier, I did become a nurse. The process of evaluating your educational goals and developing a plan based on assessment and setting goals and objectives will help us to make the best possible decision. The process will assist us through the maze of choices available to anyone today who decides to pursue education. No one should go to school because that is they only work available. One should not have to pursue a specific type of education because that is the only type of work their family does. One should know or that they can pursue their dreams even though they may have to move to find the type of education opportunities that are not readily available to them in their current location. Taking the time to read a book written by April Naha Norhanian, called *College Is For Suckers: The First College Guide You Should Read*[34] will shed some insightful perspectives on the potential student. However, I do add I hope you figure it out so you are not in school forever as I was.

> **Time Management Outcome – Find Your Time by Making Good Choices in Deciding on College/Technical Work**
>
> It takes time to pursue educational goals whether it be learning how to play the piano or obtaining a major degree in order to pursue work. Developing an educational plan will save you time as you pursue your goals and objectives. Years ago, you went through school and got an education. As you live longer, you will have many opportunities to seek out additional learning opportunities. Taking the time to plan what it is you want to do with the time you spend on educational pursuits will help you understand what it is that will help you have a happy and prosperous life. Using the quality improvement model teaches you to look at options. When one option doesn't bring the outcome desired, you need to be persistent in seeking out options to use your time wisely.

Going to Class

So now that you have decided to take a class or a series of classes to obtain a certification or diploma, let's talk about the actual classes you will be taking/attending. I have sat in lot of classes in my lifetime. I have had teachers who slapped a ruler across my fingers for talking in class to teachers who made unrealistic assignments in books that were not easily available to his students. Some classrooms have been interesting and many have not. I have taken classes in old university buildings I had to drive to at night. I have parked long distances from the classroom. I have walked in the cold to get to the class and drove home crying because I did not understand why I was not able to grasp the lesson. I have had classes that had well-defined outlines that explained exactly what was going to happen during each class period. I have had teachers who simply seemed to "wing" it flitting around from one topic to another without much of their lecture making sense. I have asked questions in all these classes. I found many times the questions were not welcomed by the teacher since the questions were not only a reflection on my inability to understand what was presented but also a reflection on the teacher's ability to present the material. There are many struggles when you decide to do something to improve yourself. So where are you at in the process?

Assess

- Are you interested in taking a class to get a better job or to learn something new in retirement?
- What class (es) are you taking now?
- Are you taking any of these classes online?
- What did you know about the class before you decided to sign up for it?
- Were there any prerequisites needed to take this class?
- What books or other tools do you need to attend the class?

Plan

Deciding to take a class may be one of several requirements needed for a professional career or it may be an opportunity to pursue an interest you have held for your entire life. I can't tell you how many times I was still looking for the books when the class started rather than reading the first assignment. Taking some time to prepare for a class prior to it starting will contribute to completion of the class. What steps are you taking to complete your next class?

Goal - long range:

- Completion of class first time

Objective(s) - future condition(s):

- To discuss goals with family and children
- To identify what prerequisites are needed for the class
- To identify what books or tools are needed for the class
- To learn about the teacher/facilitator in advance of the class
- To identify where the class is going to be held

Find Your Time: Assess, Plan, Do, Check, Review

Performance Indicator(s) - current condition(s):

- Number of classes attended by month

Do

Attending classes is a very disciplined activity, especially if the class has you sitting at your computer at your home and you are doing the class online. Sure, you don't have to drive to a classroom and you can do the class anytime you want to, but you still have to carve out time to do the class. Accomplishing the tasks related to the class becomes more difficult if you have a full-time or part-time job or a family that desires or needs a lot of attention. It is important to realize that if you are in school and you are married and/or have children, that as you prepare to take classes, you will need the support of your significant other in order to be successful in the class. Having a discussion in advance of starting the class will work out many of the annoyances with them having to change something in their schedule because your are attending a class and you need to change the support you had previously given to them. Doing a check sheet here helps to review whether you are ready to go to class see Table 9 below.

Table 9 – Check Sheet for Class Preparation

Dates	Preparation Activity	Notes
	Discuss goals with spouse/children	
	Obtain books needed	
	Obtain tools needed	
	Goggle teacher/facilitator and learn something about them, try LinkedIn	
	Find location of school	
	Find location of class	
	Need for online researching or e-mail capacity to contact other students or teacher	
	Call day of first class to make sure nothing has changed	

Check

Coming prepared to start a class lets the teacher/facilitator know that you are serious about what you are doing and that you plan to be an active participant in the process. Having the materials and demonstrating a little excitement about attending a class is infectious for all. Are you eager to attend the class? Then the class is probably right for you and you are ready to start.

Review

After you have attended the first class or two, take an hour or two and really look at whether attending the class is going to be worth your time. Does the teacher/facilitator meet your expectations? Do you have a good understanding of what the assignments will be for this class? Do you know what the evaluation process is? Have you learned anything that has you rethinking that perhaps that this class is not for you? Once you have resolved all these issues and you have decided to proceed then it is time to dig in and do the necessary work to complete the class. Are you a little scared or unsure? Be sure not to "jump ship" unless you can come up with concrete serious reasons why you have discovered this class is not for you.

Find Your Time: Assess, Plan, Do, Check, Review

> **Time Management Outcome – Find Your Time by Going to Classes**
>
> Completion of education goals requires attending classes. Figuring out early in the process what classes are needed and attending classes are great first steps in attaining an educational goal. Time spent in figuring out which educational pursuits you need and then taking slow, deliberate steps towards the overall goal will save time. In other words, if you are not sure, maybe you should wait until you really know and understand what it is you want to do.

Completing Requirements/Assignments for Classes

Every class has requirements and/or assignments that need completion. Most of us learn in chunks of time, where we digest material with some order. So do you have a current assignment that you are working on? Let's look at a few questions to learn what can help one be successful in the process.

Assess
- Did you get a course outline or syllabus or other means to know what the expectations of the class are?
- Are there any materials or other supplies needed to complete this requirement/assignment?
- Do you need a computer or a word processing program? Is there ink in your printer?
- Do you know how to ask questions of the teacher outside of the classroom by appointment or by e-mail?
- Do you have a good sense of how much time you will need to be able to complete the requirement/assignment? Do you anticipate that you will be able to complete the requirement/assignment in the allotted time?

- Do you have a strategy in place should some life event occur that makes it difficult for you to complete the requirement/assignment?

Plan

The class is scheduled – carving out your time, even starting your schedule one week in advance of the actual class may help you find unanticipated glitches. Even though there were times when the classes were difficult, it was even more difficult to find the time to do the homework that was associated with the class. I obtained my last degree by doing all the work on my home computer, interacting with my professor through the Internet, writing eight major documents and a thesis. I wrote hundreds of e-mails. I thought I had discipline when I started the process. However, I have to admit now that it is over I did not manage my time well. Having all the latitude to do the work when I wanted to do it also gave me lots of latitude to make excuses for not doing something on any given day.

It was easy when I was in nurses training where I spent time in a secluded environment in a dorm before I had the responsibilities of a marriage and children. Much of that training was about how to follow rules set up by the school to condition an individual to do what others told one to do. Remember, it was the 60s and you could not even be married and be in the nursing school, so think "controlled environment."

I was curious when I started this book to see if anyone had put together anything about how to study. I was pleasantly surprised when I found a website prepared by William J. Rapaport. Professor Rapaport is associated with the Department of Computer Science and Engineering at the State University of New York at Buffalo. You will find *How to Study: A Brief Guide*[35] at http://www.cse.buffalo.edu/~rapaport/howtostudy.html. Professor Rapaport provides excellent recommendations for anyone faced with assignments and who wants some help. I believe the guide would serve as a good *How to Study for Dummies* book. Comic strips lace the material to help make relevant points. Faced with an assignment, don't miss this free website. If you know a student faced with assignments, be sure to pass the website link along to them.

Goal - long range:

- Successful completion of requirements/assignments the first time around

Objective(s) - future condition(s):

- To be able to complete requirements/assignments on established timeline
- To be able to seek help when there are problems with completing requirements/assignments within an established timeline
- To have a strategy if some life event should occur that makes accomplishing completion of the requirements/assignments difficult

Performance Indicator(s) - current condition(s):

- Number of requirements/assignments completed by week or month (depending on time frame of class)

Do

This is a situation where setting up a check sheet will be useful. You can take a plain piece of paper and make six columns. Make a table labeling the six columns: number, requirements/assignments, description of what needs to be done, resources available to help, interim deadline date, and final deadline date (see Table 10 below). Numbering the requirements/assignments will help you visually grasp how many tasks need to be completed. Give the requirement/assignment a distinct name or label. In 10 words or less, describe the requirement/assignment. Under the resources heading, determine what you need and note whether you have those items. Given the time deadline for the assignment, put in an interim deadline. The interim deadline challenges you to complete the requirements/assignments before the final deadline. The final deadline is the date that the requirements/assignments when the last chance to get material to the teacher ends.

Table 10 – Sample Check Sheet for Class Requirements/Assignments for Class

Number	Requirements/ Assignments	Description of What Needs to be Done	Resources Available to Help	Interim Deadline Date	Final Deadline Date

Check

Now that you have mapped out all the needed requirements/assignments, and depending on the size of the class and the temperament of the teacher/facilitator, you could review the timeline check sheet with the teacher/facilitator. Be sure to put all the interim deadlines, as well as, the final deadline for all the numbers in your calendar system. See yourself completing the requirements/assignments. Visualization will not get the task done. You must start to take steps towards your goal and objectives, always keeping the interim and the final deadline dates in front of you.

Review

It is important to put two additional dates on your calendar, one date is halfway through the class and the second one is one week before the class is over. Sit back and congratulate yourself if you have completed the assignments. If something has gotten in your way, it will be a good time to regroup and look at options to get the assignments completed. Ongoing monitoring of your progress will lead to your success.

> **Time Management Outcome – Find Your Time by Completing Assignments for Classes**
>
> Completing an assignment is like putting one foot in front of the other, taking one-step at a time to get from one place to another. It takes discipline to complete one assignment after another, especially when it is hard for you to understand the value of studying the material. However, with time, taking these steps leads to completion of a class or classes and obtaining your long-range educational goal, which may lead you to a new job, or a different job, or to a job, that enriches your life.

See Appendix A for suggested performance indicators for education. While you can use Microsoft Word 2003 or Microsoft Excel 2003 to develop this form, paper and pencil will accomplish the same goal of recording information on a monthly basis. Appendix B provides additional suggestions for aspects of the education dimension where you can explore using the quality improvement model to make changes you desire in your life. The Selected Resources Section provides reference materials to help you as you develop your plan. Now that we have evaluated and put in place better systems for the educational dimension, let's evaluate the hobbies dimension.

Hobbies

Okay now that we have gotten so many other things in our life under control, we can now start to play. There are hundreds of different hobbies. In the hobby dimension, I will provide information on a hobby that has value for everyone; demonstrates what happens when one has many hobbies she enjoys and only has so much time; and the energy that occurs when a hobby becomes a component of work. Using the quality improvement model three situations are reviewed: learning how to sew, choosing between options when looking at hobbies, and discovering persistence when you decide to write. For me, I never had time for my hobbies, as is evidenced from my sewing area and the stacks of cloth bought over the last 20 years, the keyboard sitting silently in the guest room, and the unfinished book drafts. While I made enough money to buy all the equipment needed to do hobbies, I never found much time to get around to doing them. Moreover, even today in retirement, I am still struggling to get to do those things that I really want to do. I know most people have a visceral response when it comes to asking them if they would like to learn how to sew. They are either very intrigued by the possibility or shun the idea entirely. Let's look at learning to sew as an exercise in learning any new hobby because the process is similar for all.

Learning How to Sew

Sewing is a hobby, but it also is a valuable skill to mend clothes or shorten pants or make a surprise gift for someone. You may know how to sew and are enjoying the benefits of sewing; you are one of the lucky ones. Learning how to sew is not only fun, it can save you time. You can find fabric for new pillows to match your living room. You can make the pillows faster than you can find a commercially prepared covered pillow that matches what you see in your mind. Let's start with a few simple questions.

Assess

- Do you have any interest in sewing?
- Has anyone ever shown you how to thread a needle?
- Have you ever set up a sewing machine to sew a seam?
- Do you want to learn how to make simple repairs?
- Are you interested in sewing your own clothes?
- Do you want to learn how to make simple pillows, tablecloths, or napkins for your next dinner party?

Plan

If you have never threaded a needle or set up a sewing machine, don't be afraid, these tasks are easy. In addition, if you are just starting, then you want to learn a few things at a time. Sewing requires touching fabric and using simple tools. It requires lots of hand-eye coordination. You can see directly the results of your planning as the project comes together. You learn that you measure twice and cut once. Let's say you are a never-ever-done-it sewer or at best, a beginning seamstress. Everything is about fabric, thread, patterns, and tools. A sewing machine, while not essential for sewing, will make the experience more fun. To begin sewing, the simpler the sewing machine the better the choice. The more expensive machines just have more bells and whistles. A starting sewing machine can be purchased for as little as $150 new and a used machine can be picked up from Craigslist for even less. In addition, if you buy a secondhand sewing machine, be sure that you get to hear it run before you purchase it. Be sure if you buy a used machine and are new to sewing that the purchase includes the sewing manual. There is a very good reference that will help you on your quest to learn how to sew. *Teach Yourself Visually Sewing* is an excellent book for someone who wants to learn how to sew. When I want to learn a new topic, I take a book like *Teach Yourself Visually Sewing* by Debbie Colgrove[36] and read it cover to cover before I do anything. I find that in this book there are easy-to-read chapters on issues related to learning how to sew: sewing machine basics, sewing tools, fabrics, etc. You may be lucky enough to find a seamstress that is willing to show you how to sew or you could sign up for a class, but these may add expenses that are not necessary for learning how to sew. Check out http://sewing.about.com. Go to http://www.youtube.com and type in "sewing lessons" and you will find many videos that are fun to view. The point is there are many ways that you can learn how to sew, including: books, videos, and sewing lessons at fabric stores, or from your grandma.

Goal - long range:

- Sew one article

Objective(s) - future condition(s):

- To find a sewing machine to use for one month
- To purchase one yard of fabric
- To purchase one spool of thread
- To gather tools needed to measure fabric and to cut it
- To find one simple pattern to make, such as a pillow cover

Performance Indicator(s) - current condition(s):

- Completion of one article per month

Do

Take an afternoon, after you have read the *Teach Yourself Visually Sewing* book, and get started by learning about the sewing machine you are going to use. Years ago, I belonged to 4-H. I don't remember much about the program except that I made a yellow skirt that had straps and Judy, my husband's cousin, made a white dress with red trim. My yellow skirt didn't fit too well and the trim on Judy's dress bled though to the white fabric. We both laugh about these little catastrophes now but both of us have enjoyed a lifetime of sewing projects. Take out the pattern or directions to sew a pillow cover, cut out the fabric, and sew it up according to the directions. Just do it! Don't worry about it being perfect. Ask questions of someone you know who sews if you find you are not sure what to do. Soon you will be showing your friends your creations. As you increase in your sewing skill building, you will find that you are on a continuum from beginning seamstress to master seamstress. You will find that you can develop a check sheet for each project you take on to assist you in the process. Eventually, you will be able to assemble what you need easily and will be sewing up one project after another.

Check

Be sure to give yourself time and a few small goals to work toward before you start making clothes for yourself or curtains for your bedroom. Gradually increase the projects you take on. Soon you will be increasing in your confidence as to what you are able to do. Sewing, or any hobby, helps you have fun at the same time. It helps you build your self-esteem and provides you with something to talk about and maybe even to brag about.

Review

Finding someone who either wants to learn sewing along with you, or someone who knows how to sew that can become your sewing friend, is helpful, especially if their skill level is a little ahead of where you are. If you sew and you know someone that is interested in learning, take the time to show them how to start. Think of the fun you can have with your granddaughter and one of her friends as they come to your home to learn how to sew on the old sewing machine that is sitting idle.

> **Time Management Outcome – Find Your Time by Learning How to Sew**
>
> To be able to sew a hem on a pair of pants or to sew a torn seam can give life back to a garment and can save you lots of time in finding its replacement. To be able to sew a new blouse gets you one that fits in the color and design that you want. While you spend some time finding the pattern and cloth, cutting it out and sewing it up, you save all the time in going from one store to another looking for just what you want. Many times, you can not find your size or the color does not match the rest of the outfit. Besides, many find sewing is relaxing and beats fighting the traffic to get to the stores and standing in line to pay for commercially made clothing.

Choosing Between Options When Looking at Hobbies

There is now more time in the schedule, as some of the routine aspects of life have gotten under better control from a time management perspective. We have many options available to us as we look at the hobbies that may interest us. While I have many established hobbies, like sewing, I have always wanted to play the piano. I really want to play a song from my childhood that my mom played on the family piano called "Deep Purple." Therefore, I start with the quality improvement model and I assess where I am. I will add more detail that is personal so the reader can see how we can be stuck and not do something we are interested in doing with our lives. The quality improvement model is used as a guide to bring some order to the chaos and to focus me on something I think I really want to do and to learn how to put this activity into my schedule.

Assess

- Do I have the time to learn how to play the piano?

- How much musical training have I had?
- Do I have the time to practice?
- Do I own a keyboard?
- How am I going to learn?

Plan

I am retired. I have extra time. I do want to learn how to play the piano. I remember hearing my mom play the piano from time to time and listening to the old phonograph play records. I sang in the church choir when I was young. Plugging a headset into my ears and listening to music has always been a soothing relaxation for me.

Therefore, I look over the situation and here is where I find I am. I have a keyboard – in fact, it is my second keyboard. I bought the first one in 1986 after my mom passed away. It was somehow my connection to her. I had the keyboard in the living room for a long time, and then it was in the closet. I never took the time to play it very much.

One day a couple years later, at Costco, I saw a fancier keyboard. It had extra features and even had a way for me to learn by following the colored lights. I became engaged with trying to find methods for me to learn that would meet my needs to do it "my way." I tried two or three different "learn how to play the piano software programs" and soon became bored or overwhelmed with the information. I really could not figure it out. I tried a class at the local community college but could never find the time to practice.

I moved the keyboard into the guest bedroom. The grandchildren would turn it on, play a few notes, and generally leave on the blinking red lights, but I never really sat down to learn how to play. Recently, again at Costco, I found some books that were for beginners who wanted to learn how to play the piano and they had instructions. I read the instructions and they indicated I needed to go to the keyboard and practice, not just read! So what was getting in my way of practicing and what could I do about it?

Sandie Barrie

Well I looked at the psychological aspects – I did want to do it. Was I afraid that I could not do it or was I afraid that I might not be successful? Was I overwhelmed by the thought of the time I would spend practicing that might not produce something tangible? I did not come from a family that played instruments. I perceived that my husband would not find it valuable that I wanted to learn how to play the piano. I realized I never spoke to him about my desire to play the piano. I really did not need his permission, blessing or help to learn how to play. I had to admit this was a weak excuse. The most important thing I needed to do was just start. However, there was always an excuse. I was stuck in the preparation stage of change.

As I sat at the computer writing this part of the book, I realized that I really was not interested much in what was on television anymore and that each evening after supper, I could find some time to practice since my husband generally went and watched television. Therefore, I promised myself that I would start today.

The goal is broad and doesn't really get me started so I wrote a few objectives to go along with the goal.

Goal - long range:

- Play the piano

Objective(s) - future condition(s):

- Complete a lesson a month in *How to Read Music In 3 Easy Lessons*[37] by spending two hours per week on doing the exercises provided by using the DVDs, reading the book, and hitting the keys on the keyboard

- Complete a chapter a week in *Learn to Play the Piano and Keyboard: A Step-by-Step Guide*[38] by spending two hours per week on doing the exercises provided by using the DVDs, reading the book, and hitting the keys on the keyboard

<u>Performance Indicator(s) - current condition(s):</u>

- Number of hours playing the piano per month

Do

The "do" component of the model seemed easy. Sit at the piano and hit the keys. I would take the two books that I had purchased at Costco and would spend time each week with the material sitting at my keyboard. It excited me to realize there were DVDs to help me with the process.

Check

In order to hold myself accountable to my new goal and objectives, I first scheduled time on my calendar to remind myself to complete my tasks identified in the "do" section. Below are my actual check sheets for the first two weeks. In addition, the next six weeks are all blank.

Table 11 – Check Sheet for Learning How to Play the Piano

	S	M	T	W	T	F	S	S	M	T	W	T	F	S
Read Music		10			5									
Play the Piano		20			15									

Sandie Barrie

Review

Every day at 7 p.m., I get a message that reminds me that I want to play the piano. I am ignoring the message but leaving it on my calendar for now to remind me that when I get a few more things off my plate, I still do want to learn how to play the piano. Knowing that I really do not have enough time to practice each day, I have decided to wait until I have the time so that I do not get discouraged since I have come to realize that I must practice to learn how to play.

> **Time Management Outcome – Find Your Time by Choosing Between Options When Looking at Hobbies**
>
> While I have left the date with myself on my daily calendar, I have concluded that I have to choose between my hobbies that I enjoy doing. Learning how to play the piano is still is on my "Bucket List" (things I want to do in my lifetime) but I need to get a few more things out of the way before I will have the time to devote to the practice needed to learn how to play the piano.

Discovering Persistence When You Decide To Write

I really like to write. In fact, I like to write enough that I put this situation in the hobby dimension rather than the work dimension. I have dreamed of writing books for years. However, I have never written a book for sale. I woke up one morning about eight months into my retirement and said, "*Okay, so what am I going to do with the rest of my life?*" I said, "*Okay, I want to write a couple of books.*" I have several drafts of books. I started one years ago on a Selectric typewriter in the 1970s. I had tossed the titles around for a couple of years and had tested them out on my family and friends. The first working title was called *Forty*

Years in the Life of a Nurse and the second one was called *Lessons Learned From the Men in My Life*. I have drafts for both books and a couple on sewing. Now, I find myself with a draft of a book about time management coming together and even though I have received a lot of satisfaction from the pure activity of sitting at the computer and doing the writing, I want to get it published. For most of my life, publishing a book was something that just was not available to the ordinary individual who had a family and a job and commitments.

Therefore, I decided that I needed to use the Time Management Template shared in Section 7 to get this book published so that I could move the typed words on the computer into a book for sale. I was stalling and finding other reasons for not finishing the book and getting it out for sale. It helped when I changed my thinking from *"no one would want to read this"* to *"this is valuable information that could help others."* I started by asking myself questions.

Assess

- How long was it going to take to finish the book?
- Was the young copy editor that I had met at my last job going to have time to take the mistakes in grammar out of the draft?
- What kind of format was I going to sell the book in – as a perfect bound book or as an e-Book?
- How was I going to market the book?
- How long was I going to take to get a final draft into a sellable product?

Plan

I had a good draft but there were still parts that were not complete. I seem to like to jump around when I write. When I am stuck, I hop around in the document until I find a part where I want to write. I also found a major problem in the structure of information within the document. I needed to locate the young graduate whom I had met at my last job. I knew that if I set a tone of need for her to do some work for me that would help to motivate me to get the work done. I decided I needed to print the draft out and evaluate what was not complete. I realized that I was spending a lot of time trying to perfect the document myself rather than admitting to myself that every writer needs an editor.

Sandie Barrie

I had taken a class from the Small Business Development Center on writing a business plan. In writing the business plan, I had focused on selling a book over the Internet that turned out in 2006 to be possible but not well developed. I dug around until I found the business plan, dusted it off, and realized that I had put a lot of work into writing that document over a several-month period. Nevertheless, at the time, I had not retired and still had the obligations of my "day job."

I wrote a simple goal and objectives.

<u>Goal - long range:</u>

- Publish book, *Find Your Time: Assess, Plan, Do, Check, Review*

<u>Objective(s) - future condition(s):</u>

- To print out document and determine what needs to be done to complete the book weekly
- To negotiate with copy editor to review the book
- To begin to evaluate marketing opportunities weekly

<u>Performance Indicator(s) - current condition(s):</u>

- Publish book by August 15, 2009

Do

I tracked the new graduate down and found her in Grass Valley, CA. Lucky for me I found she was available to do some work for me. We sent a couple of e-mails back and forth and agreed on a fee and amount of time to accomplish the work. I sent an e-mail off to the Nevada Small Business Development Center and found the man I had taken the class from was still working there. He recommended that I meet with a marketing specialist on his staff. I found that I had met this person back in 2006 and so I was hoping she remembered whom I was. I prepared an agenda for the meeting and sent it to her in advance of the meeting. We renewed our relationship, which had previously been positive. At the meeting, I started through the agenda that helped both of us keep on track. I told her what steps I had taken to establish myself as a small business. I told her I wanted to sell a book on the Internet. I shared with her the costs of selling the book on the Internet. I shared a copy of the book's table of contents. I gave her a brief overview of how the book shared information on change theory and a quality improvement model and applied the information to 10 life dimensions that affect us in our lives. I told her that I really needed her help to focus my available marketing dollars. To my surprise and delight, I found that the university was planning a conference on interactive marketing media and that there were other resources available at the Nevada Small Business Development Center to get me started. She further suggested that I do research on the topic of thought leadership in concert with learning more about blogs. I went home and signed up for the seven-hour conference for $25, scheduled in three weeks. The paper was starting to build on my desk with drafts of the book, information about the business requirements, and research on blogs. I decided that I needed a call-up file to keep me organized. I was trying to manage too much stuff in my head. I put some appointments into my calendar to keep me on track. In addition, off I went and just started at moving towards self-publishing this book. It is interesting to see that once you start some movement toward a goal, things just seem to happen.

I developed a simple plan (see Table 12 below) of the things I needed to do and when I wanted to see them accomplished by to make sure that I could reach my goal. I put the plan in my purse since I knew that I would be traveling over the next couple of weeks and I did not want to forget what I was committing to do as I sat in front of the computer dreaming of getting my book published.

Table 12 – Abbreviated Draft Weekly Goal Sheet for Self-Publishing Book

Week	Book Draft	Marketing	Business
3/10	Write every day on book draft	Read and do an hour a day from Dave Evans' book, *Social Media Marketing: An Hour a Day*[39]	Get an Employer ID Number (EIN) and obtain S-Corporation status
3/17	Write every day on book draft	Do exercises in book – Join Facebook	Set-up business checking account
3/21	Write every day on book draft.	Do exercises in book – Join LinkedIn	Get a business license
3/28	Write every day on book draft	Do exercises in book – Join Twitter	Get sales tax forms
4/4	Write every day on book draft	Meet with staff at Small Business Development Center – learn about marketing	Meet with staff at Small Business Development Center - starting a business
4/11	Write every day on book draft	Attend local conference on social media	Complete budget planning
4/18	Write every day on book draft	Develop website	Study IRS "Starting a Business and Keeping Records"
4/25	Write every day on book draft	Develop shop cart	Set up phone lines
5/2	Negotiate with copy editor	Figure out how to do a blog	Set up business e-mail address
5/9	Copy editor review	Write text for blog	Maintain budget
5/16	Obtain ISBN and copyright	Write text for blog	Maintain budget
6/23	Receive comments back from copy editor and finalize book draft	Write text for blog and make announcement of book release	Maintain budget
7/30	Load document to PDF and place on website	Put up website with shop cart and blog http://www.findyourtime.org	Get ready for the sales to roll in through the Internet to my bank account and start to pay taxes ;-)
8/6	Monitor e-mail for issues related to website function	Reread Dave Evans book, *Social Media Marketing: An Hour a Day*	Continue to review revenues versus expenses

Check

As I moved through the process of setting up a business, writing the book, and learning about marketing, I found that I was making adjustments in the book examples and the options I decided to use in the book. One example would be that instead of putting the print-on-demand book to a third party, I decided to publish it myself using my own website, www.findyourtime.org , which was a big savings for me since I would not have to pay fees to a third party. I began to feel like I should have put this project in the work dimension rather than the hobby dimension. I got so excited about the possibilities for marketing and social media that I just wanted to learn about those topics rather than complete the writing of the book. Social media became a huge distraction as I learned about Facebook, LinkedIn, and Twitter. However, for years, I have been writing early in the day and because I had a disciplined habit to perform this task, I just had to be sure that I opened up the book file before I went to the iGoogle page to see what was new on the social media sites I was watching. The beauty of the quality improvement model is that with time, it becomes a way of thinking. Setting an actual goal with objectives and when one starts taking steps one after another, success occurs. Success will occur, especially if persistence is a core skill that is part of your personality.

Review

You know I was successful if you have the book or the downloadable document in your hands and are finding out some ideas about change theory and the quality improvement model and how to apply it to your life dimensions. If you have a story of your own that you want to write, take the time to find out about self-publishing and you can do it. I am writing a book about my self-publishing adventures during the last six months… If you think you are interested check out my website at www.findyourtime.org.

> **Time Management Outcome – Find Your Time by Discovering Persistence When You Decide to Write**
>
> I am not sure if one can actually learn persistence. Being persistent probably is something that just happens with some people and doesn't happen with other people. I am lucky that, for whatever reason, when I put my mind to something, I can do it once I determine that I want to do it. The game is finding the resources, the time, and the skills to accomplish it. As you evaluate your use of time, it is important to realize that goals and objectives desired will not necessarily happen in an instant, or even overnight, but may take time, and in some cases, a lot of time to figure out. Nevertheless, success can occur for many needs and/or wants in your life if you remain persistent in your endeavors, and learn how to use your time wisely.

See Appendix A for suggested performance indicators for hobbies. While you can use Microsoft Word 2003 or Microsoft Excel 2003 to develop this form, paper and pencil will accomplish the same goal of recording information on a monthly basis. Appendix B provides additional suggestions for aspects of the hobby dimension where you can explore using the quality improvement model to make changes you desire in your life. The Selected Resources Section provides reference materials to help you as you develop your plan. Now that we have evaluated and put in place better systems for the hobby dimension, let's evaluate the service opportunities dimension.

Find Your Time: Assess, Plan, Do, Check, Review

Service Opportunities

We all like to help others – as they say, "to pay it forward" when we are able. Many of us also feel that we just do not have the time to contribute or to volunteer and to give up our time. What you have learned in using the quality improvement model in other dimensions of your life is that you are able to create time to do some of the things you want to do when you learn how to use your time better. Additionally, if you use the quality improvement model, you are able to organize your service projects in such a way that you can maximize the time spent and leave a legacy behind you. You do not want to waste your time in what you do with your volunteer life. Using the quality improvement model, three situations are examined in the service opportunities dimension: writing proposals for short-term projects, maximizing energy in long-term projects, and building on using groups of people in accomplishing lifelong projects.

Writing Proposals for Short-term Projects

Over the years of my professional life, I had to write many proposals, especially when I was working as the director of the case management department in a large urban hospital. I had many dreams to make the system to work better. I had to write them up for upper management to review. Let me make it clear from the start that not all these proposals were success stories and not all were accepted, but some rather major changes in policy did occur because I wrote a proposal. In this situation, you will realize that by putting the ideas down on paper and asking for a review by decision makers, you can save a lot of time. The following idea was a dream and, as you will see, it was an unrealized one, but I am getting ahead of the story, so let's proceed with a few questions and some background.

Assess

- How can a hobby turn into an opportunity to raise money as a volunteer activity?
- How can I use my time to support two nonprofit organizations that could use my help at the same time?

Plan

As you know, my dad was a florist. I learned at a very young age how to tie a floral bow. I like to handle the pretty, colorful ribbon and everyone needs bows for the Christmas holidays. Recently, I had the opportunity to work with the Statewide Volunteer Organization. The Statewide Volunteer Organization is a nonprofit organization that tries to match individuals who want to volunteer with nonprofit organizations that need volunteers to accomplish their missions. The Statewide Volunteer Organization Business Plan needed financial resources to broaden the scope of its work and to help pay for the computer program and the staff needed to support the matching process. At about the same time, the church I attend announced it needed crafts for its annual Christmas bazaar, where the money was going to be used to further church goals.

Being the right-brained person that I am, I merged the two needs together in my mind. I got the idea for making bows and for selling them at the church Christmas bazaar and splitting half the profit with the church and half with the Statewide Volunteer Organization. The whole project seemed so easy to me. I would make pretty bows and offer them for sale at the church Christmas bazaar. I would split the profit between the two organizations. I wrote up the proposal, listing out the expense for the ribbon and projecting the number of bows that would sell. I expected in the end to share about $348 each with the two organizations.

I started the process by sending the chairperson of the church bazaar a proposal and asking her to sign an agreement that stated that half of the profit would go to the Statewide Volunteer Organization and half to the church (see Figure 4 below).

> *Connie, the last time I did bows for the Christmas bazaar was when we were still in the old church – so it's been a few years. I could not make them in the past few years because I had to have hand surgery. Well, the hand is well and I have the time to make bows.*
>
> *In my retirement, I have been working with the Statewide Volunteer Organization, which is a nonprofit organization that works to increase volunteerism in all community areas: church, nonprofits, youth, and government.*
>
> *Briefly, I would like to make bows. I would like to sell them at the Anywhere Christmas Bazaar with one-half of the amount that is made (after the cost of the ribbon, wires and picks has been subtracted) would be donated to the Statewide Volunteer Organization and one-half to the Anywhere Church (check to be written by Anywhere Church to Statewide Volunteer Organization). Of course, I would donate my time to make the bows, as well as, the time I would be at the Christmas bazaar selling the bows. Two helpers will assist me on December 7th. By splitting the profit, the Statewide Volunteer Organization would then use the money to buy small ads to put in church bulletins in the community. The purpose of the ads would be to let the congregants learn about a website where they can match up their skills with volunteer needs in the community. On December 7th, I would plan to actually make bows for people so they can see how they are made, allowing customers to get exactly the size they need.*
>
> *If you remember, the bows were a hit! I will take the risk of paying for any unused ribbon and/or bows that don't sell since I am so confident that I can get them all gone by the end of the day.*
>
> *I am proposing to make 250 bows (or more, if you think they would sell) since I am sure that the Christmas bazaar has grown. The bows would sell at an average of $4.05 per bow since I would want to make some small bows for use in small containers, some medium bows to use on potted plants, and some large bows to use on wreaths. If I am to make 250 bows, it will take me a few days so that I do not overuse my hand in the process. I need approval of this proposal to move forward. I want to go to Costco where I purchase most of the ribbon while they still have a good selection.*
>
> *On average, the small bolt of ribbon can make 50 bows and costs $10; the middle bolt of ribbon can make 15 bows and costs $7; and the large bolt of ribbon can*

make 12 bows and costs $7. Here is my breakdown of revenue and expenses with the net profit. See the budget for the Christmas Bows Proposal below.

Revenues	Items	
	50 small bows $1.50 per bow (blue dot)	$75
	75 medium bows $3.00 per bow (yellow dot)	$225
	125 large bows $5.00 per bow (red dot)	$625
Total		$925
Expenses	2 small bolt (2 yd per bow) @ $10 ea	$20
	15 medium bolts (1 yd 1ft per bow) @ $7 ea	$105
	12 large bolts (4 yd per bow from 50 yd bolt) @ $7 ea	$84
	Picks and wire	$10
Total		$229
Net Profit	Net Profit to be split between Anywhere Church and Statewide Volunteer Organization	$696
Total	Amount to be donated to each organization (1/2 Net Profit)	$348

Note: The prices are very reasonable since large craft store bows are $9.99 and $12.99, and medium-sized bows are $6.99 at local commercial stores.

In order to make this work, I will purchase the ribbon and carry the expense until the church can issue a check to me post-event for the cost of the ribbon.

I will place a small colored dot on each bow. The dot serves to demonstrate how many bows sold. I will present that paper to you post-event along with a full accounting of revenue and expenses.

As I mentioned, Statewide Volunteer Organization would use the donation to further their mission to match potential volunteers with nonprofit organizations. One option could be purchasing ad space in church bulletins. Karen has advised me that the cost of a space in Anywhere Church bulletin is $120 per year or $60 for six months. The amount the Statewide Volunteer Organization receives could purchase five different church ads for a six-month period. The Anywhere Church actually receives the money back and invests in volunteerism.

If this proposal is acceptable, please sign below and return to me in the self-addressed stamped envelope and I will go purchase the ribbon and start making the bows and place the event on my calendar. If you should have any questions, please give me a call at 000-0000.

Name of Church Coordinator: _____ Date: _____

Sandie Barrie: _____ Date: _____
Keep original and send a copy back to Sandie

Figure 4. Proposal - Christmas Bows for Anywhere Christmas Bazaar on December 7, 2008

Goal - long range:

- Maximize my time to help provide funding to two nonprofit organizations

Objective(s) - future condition(s):

- Number of dollars to be contributed to church bazaar and Statewide Volunteer Organization

Performance Indicator(s) - current condition(s):

- Written proposal to gain approval prior to completing work

Do

A few days went by, and while at church, I ran into the chairperson who told me that she already had bows. I then asked if I could do other floral arrangements – again, with the idea of splitting the profit between the two organizations. Then she let me know that the ladies guild charter did not allow such sharing to occur. There was no need for a check sheet here since no activity took place.

Check

I saved time because I determined that making bows or floral arrangements was not going to meet my needs to see that both organizations received some of the fruits of my work. It did not work since the church guild needed all the monies made from the church bazaar to go directly to the church goals.

Review

I do think it is a great idea to use one's hobby to engage in working with several organizations to help them all out. I share the idea in this book on time management because it is a good, practical way of collaborating to benefit two organizations. I wanted to accomplish two goals to help two different nonprofit organizations, one that had limited means to raise money for its goals. One problem I realized is that I wrote a lengthy proposal. I believe I may have had more success if I had written a more succinct proposal. I knew how to do that since I wrote many of them when I worked in one of my previous jobs. The basic format for a SOPPADA is in Appendix 3. Maybe next year I can start a little earlier with the church bazaar chairperson and work closer with others on the bazaar committee so they see the value of the money coming to their organization as well as the support that can be given to another nonprofit organization who does not have the same resource capacity to raise monies.

> **Time Management Outcome – Find Your Time by Writing Proposals for Short-term Projects**
>
> It is important to realize that not every time you think you can use your time in a wise way to accomplish noble goals that others will see it the same way. Writing down your idea in a simple proposal format allows others to determine if they want to join the effort. It can be an easy and timesaving way to get approval to move forward on projects or programs.

Maximizing Energy in Long-term Projects

Have you ever wanted to leave a legacy or do something to be able to memorialize a loved one who has passed away? Here is an idea that you can replicate that does not take much time and has an ongoing outcome of stocking the shelves of the local food bank. The seed for this idea started as I sat at a church meeting. I had decided to go to the meeting as a way to try to get out of the depression following the death of my dad. The thought was simple. If we put out some barrels, people could bring food for the local food bank to church on the third Saturday and Sunday of the month to help restock their shelves.

Assess

- What are you interested in trying to do to help another group of people?
- How do you plan to make a difference of service in your community?
- How much time do you have to accomplish what you want to do?

- How can you leverage the amount of time you spend to organize efforts that you can then leave?

Plan

Of course, there were the approvals that were needed. Therefore, I wrote a letter to the pastor of the church explaining the idea and how I was motivated to suggest this idea from the discussion that had occurred at the meeting. A little to my surprise, he approved the idea. So then, I needed to get the word out. It took me about 10 minutes to design a flier. I asked the secretary to put into the bulletin as a full-size insert, (see Figure 5 below) on the second Saturday and Sunday of each month.

Anywhere Church

Next Week at all Masses

Church Food Drive

Non-perishable food is preferred. Please bring your contribution before or after Mass. Your help is appreciated by all those who need a helping hand. Remember, high protein foods are especially appreciated. These include: peanut butter, canned meat (tuna, chicken, etc.), baby food, beans, soup with beans and meat, and powdered milk.

Food is collected at Mass, and on the following Monday, St. Vincent's picks it up. The food will be available for distribution to families in need the same week it is donated.

If you prefer to make a cash donation to St. Vincent's to help fill their shelves, a poor box is available.

Figure 5. Example Church Flier

Sandie Barrie

I like to talk so I asked for permission to make an announcement about the new program prior to each Mass. I called a local company and got four barrels. The congregants could put the food in the barrel as they came through the door. I called St. Vincent's and talked with the driver that picked up the food. I asked him to pick-up the food at Anywhere Church on the Monday following the third Saturday and Sunday of each month. The pastor encouraged all to bring a couple cans of food and place it in the barrels.

<u>Goal - long range:</u>

- Provide food to the needy

<u>Objective(s) - future condition(s):</u>

- Maintain steady flow of food for those who distribute food to the needy

<u>Performance Indicator(s) - current condition(s):</u>

- Number of pounds of food per month donated to nonprofit organization who distribute food
- Amount of cash provided per month to nonprofit organization who distribute food

Do

In just a little time, I had the permission of the pastor to conduct the food drive. The secretary helped by putting the flier in the bulletin. I spoke at each of the Masses and talked about how I was the oldest of 13 children and how there was always a need for food and how we were able to grow our own food and canned at harvest much of what we would eat during the winter months. I told the parishioners that I was getting this organized as a tribute to my dad and his ability to see that his family had food. I pointed out that in Reno, NV most people can not grow food on their property. It just was not possible to grow food on our property and that there were many people who ended up in Reno who did not have food.

Check

I sure didn't need a data collection sheet to see that the effort was a success. Over the next few months, the church secretary put the flier in the second Saturday and Sunday bulletins. The flier came out each month and the food was coming in on the third Saturday and Sunday of the month. I thought all was well until one of the ushers let me know that while the Mass was going on, people were taking the food out of the barrels, which upset many of them. Being the person I am, I thought that whoever was taking the food from the barrels must need the food. However, I found that many parishioners did not feel the same way. Therefore, we simply changed where the food was left at the church. Parishioners brought the food to the altar.

Interestingly enough, some parishioners felt this distracted from the solemnity of the Mass and disliked the appearance of sacks of food hanging around the altar during the service. The pastor quieted the remarks. He stated the food would stay at the altar. He reiterated having food at the altar was not disrespectful.

There was a lot of food around the altar. The parishioners moved the food from the altar to the door where the St. Vincent's staff picked up the food. This was an easy task to accomplish with the leadership of the pastor who picked up a bag of the food at the end of the last Mass and carried it to the side door as the rest of the parishioners followed, picking up bags and together, moving the food.

Review

Utilizing the "review" portion of the quality improvement model work by examining the results of the plan and to trigger what could be done differently to improve the process, or in this case, to duplicate the effort. Several other local churches have started similar programs. In addition, just think – if you took this idea to your church how the idea of bringing unused food from your pantry to a central collection point could expand. The individual parishioner brings a can or two of food to a central location. The nonprofit organization picks up the food and distributes the food to those who need food.

Sandie Barrie

At one of the churches, a second idea came up to collect eyeglasses. The secretary added the following to the initial flier for food, see Figure 6 below.

> Eyeglasses Needed
>
> Have your children outgrown their eyeglasses or do you have an old pair you don't need anymore? The parish will be collecting used eyeglasses next weekend. The glasses will be taken to Anywhere Optical Center and made available to someone who needs them. There will be a separate box on the altar with the food collection.

Figure 6. Ad for Eyeglasses Collection

And the beat goes on . . .

Time Management Outcome – Find Your Time by Maximizing Energy in Long-term Projects

A flier put into a church bulletin once a month has resulted in thousands of pounds of food and a couple thousand pairs of eyeglasses brought to local nonprofit organizations since 1994. My time involvement in this particular project ceased years ago. The church staff completes the few minor tasks needed monthly. A little bit of my time in getting things started has helped hundreds of people I will never meet. No one has received more than I have, knowing that such a small amount of time invested continues in my mind to honor my dad and mom who always made sure, there was food on our table.

Building on Using Groups of People in Lifelong Projects

Some service opportunities stick with us and we find ourselves going back to them repeatedly. It is 19 degrees in Reno and the television screen has pictures of thousands of people going to the volunteer center to get a warm meal at Christmastime. People like Evelyn Mount have set up their homes to receive food and then work at redistributing the food to the needy. You cannot listen to the local news year after year without hearing about Evelyn Mount – she is a model of service for everyone. She demonstrates what one person is able to do when she puts her mind and talents to work. It is impossible to count how many thousands of people in Reno have received a hot meal or a bag of groceries as the result of her work. I know that no woman wants her age in print. Let's just say that Evelyn is an old woman in generosity and a young woman in getting out and doing something that has provided service to the people of Reno-Sparks for over 30 years.

Assess

- Do you have anything that captures your interest?
- Do you see something that you would like to do year after year?
- Do you see a need that no one else is fulfilling?
- Do you have just a little amount of time that you can donate to doing something for others?
- Do you want to "pay it forward"?

Plan

Hey, how about coats, jackets, hats, and gloves? It is just an idea, but what if we decided to collect used clothes and make sure that the people who need the outside clothes get them without asking or judging why it is that they may need the clothes in the first place. It is simple to do and can be based on what we learned in the church food drive that was described earlier. The plan is simple as outlined in Figure 7 below.

Activity	Time
Send an e-mail to the church secretary to obtain permission from the pastor to hold the clothes drive December 26th and include flier and announcement	2 minutes
Develop the flier to include in the church bulletin on January 4th for clothes collection on January 10th and 11th at all Masses	10 minutes
Develop the language to include in the public statements before Masses on January 4th for clothes collection on January 10th and 11th	6 minutes
Make a big sign and put out on January 4th in plain view of the congregation as they enter the church	10 minutes
Move the sign to a safe spot for the clothes to be collected on January 10th and 11th	5 minutes
Pick up clothes at the end of Masses on January 10th and January 11th	25 minutes
Distribute clothes to nonprofit organizations on January 12th	2 to 8 hours depending on the amount of clothes received and driving distance to the nonprofit organizations (90 minutes actual)
Send a note of thanks to the church secretary by e-mail to be included in the church bulletin for the week of January 17th and 18th with number count	2 minutes
TOTAL SPENT	**150 minutes**

Figure 7. Plan to Collect Clothes 2009

Goal - long range:

- Set up annual drive for outside clothing

Objective (future condition):

- Provide clothes to nonprofit organization during time of the year when they are needed

Find Your Time: Assess, Plan, Do, Check, Review

Performance Indicator(s) - current condition(s):

- Number of outside clothes collected during January

Do

With the plan in hand, getting started on the process simply takes a few minutes depending on the time and skill you have in typing up a Word document or two. Put some dates on your calendar to remind you that you are in charge of this project. Sometimes, doing things like this just goes faster if you do the work yourself. However, if you like, you can make this a fun task for the Brownie group, your Bunco gang, or your baseball team. Examples of the flier and announcements are included below in Figure 8.

NEXT WEEK – January 10 and 11

Anywhere Church Clothes Drive

Did you get a new coat or jacket for Christmas? Do you have an extra coat or jacket hanging in the closet? Do you have any extra gloves or scarves? Adult and children's clothes are needed!!

Bring your <u>clean, usable</u> coats, jackets, hats, and gloves on Saturday, January 10 or Sunday, January 11 to any of the Masses.

Do you belong to Anywhere Church and need some warm outside clothing? Contact Sandie at 000-0000 to obtain needed clothing from the donations. All other coats, jackets, hats, and gloves will be donated to appropriate nonprofit organizations.

Figure 8. Example Flier for Clothes Drive (to be placed in church bulletin one week in advance of clothes drive)

Sandie Barrie

The first thing to do is make a sign that says, "Clothes Drive on January 10 and 11". Take the sign to the church and put it up in the foyer on January 3rd. Be sure to put it in a conspicuous spot! Find an old box, wrap it with some colorful paper, and place it under the sign. Looking around your house, you will find you probably don't need to spend a dime on this! On January 10th simply move the sign to the location where you want the clothes piled. Again, this does not require a check sheet, except you may want to take note of the amount that is collected.

Check

Total time spent in setting up the drive and taking the clothes to the nonprofit organization was 150 minutes for me. The parishioners contributed 700 pieces of clothing. The evaluation is quick and easy. Do the math, every minute spent resulted in 4.6 items collected. It was interesting that out of this 1,000-family parish, no one called and indicated they needed outside clothes for their family. WOW! Being able to "pay it forward" in this way gives purpose to my life and makes all the difference in figuring out how to use my time more efficiently, allowing me more time for these activities.

Review

Note how much was collected. Write a quick thank you to the congregation for the clothes collected. Send off to the church secretary and ask her to include in the church bulletin the week after the clothes drive. Put on your calendar for next year to remind yourself to repeat the process. Note anything that may make the process work better (see Table 13 below). Evaluate time commitments to do one extra clothes drive later in the year, maybe clothes for new moms on Mother's Day to be donated to the local hospital.

Table 13 – Evaluation of Clothes Drive Process

Phase of Process	Change Recommendations and What Worked
Preparation (time to get started)	Sending a quick e-mail to church secretary worked well; secretary redrafted the flier to make it more visually appealing. The reader did not read the announcement. Having the clothes drive done right after the holidays was good timing as opposed to doing right before the holidays.
Collection Period (one week from notice in bulletin to day clothes were brought in)	Collection period was only one week from time of notice to time of collection; I would suggest expanding the time period to two weeks and would add a second notice in the bulletin. The paper sign fell down. The parishioners did not see it.
Production (moving clothes from church to nonprofit organization)	Luckily, for me, another parishioner took one of the loads of clothes to a nonprofit organization. Next time, I will arrange to have the nonprofit organization pick up the clothes and have the clothes stored in a room at the church until they can pick up, saving me approximately 60 minutes. I did not include the destination for the clothes. Next time, I will include that the clothes will go to a nonprofit organization that distributes the clothes directly to the homeless. The homeless will not pay for the clothes.

> **Time Management Outcome – Find Your Time by Building on Groups in Lifelong Projects**
>
> The process to collect clothes does not take much time to do. Groups of people can collect clothes for the elderly in the nursing home (like white socks), for new moms who need maternity clothes, for babies born in the local hospital whose moms and dads don't have resources to buy them clothes, or toiletries for the homeless, or the water cooling neck scarves for the troops overseas.
>
> All you need is a source of people from a church or work environment, a person to take on the process of organizing the work, and someone to make sure the clothes/toiletries get to the nonprofit organizations that are set up to do the distributions. You can use your time wisely by organizing groups of people to help you in your volunteer efforts. Of course, when the bright idea comes in from one of the participants of the church, school, or workplace, the leaders need to embrace the idea and pick up the project and support it with gusto!

In summary, see Appendix A for suggested performance indicators for service opportunities. While you can use Microsoft Word 2003 or Microsoft Excel 2003 to develop this form, paper and pencil will accomplish the same goal of recording information on a monthly basis. Appendix B provides additional suggestions for aspects of the service opportunities dimension where you can explore using the quality improvement model to make changes you desire in your life. The Selected Resources Section provides reference materials to help you as you develop your plan. Now that we have evaluated and put in place better systems for the service opportunities dimension, let's evaluate the building relationships dimension.

Find Your Time: Assess, Plan, Do, Check, Review

Building Relationships

Each day of your life, you interact with someone, and that interaction is either the beginning of a new relationship, the continuation of a relationship, or the end of a relationship. The interaction brings forth communication and the main way the communication occurs is through talking. For some of us, we use sign language and some of us are just able to nod our heads. Talking is a gift that allows us to find our way through life, going to work and school. Of course, there is much more to building a relationship than talking but talking and listening are core elements required for relationships to flourish. Using the quality improvement model, three situations in the building relationships dimension are investigated: creating contacts for the family, preparing agendas when dealing with professionals, and cherishing options when making friends. Have you given much thought to the relationships in your life and the ones that come into your life because of your work situation, your church affiliation, or the people you interact with when you buy those items needed to live?

Creating Contacts for the Family

Our first relationship started with mom and dad. From the beginning, we all have taken different paths as we moved through life. We have gotten to the present point moving through hundreds of relationships. For most of us, our families of origin still hold a very special spot in our hearts. Let's not forget the in-laws that they have brought with them.

Sandie Barrie

Assess

- What kind of relationship do you have with your family of origin?
- How do you keep in contact with your family of origin?
- How much do you talk with your family of origin?
- What do you talk about with your family of origin?

Plan

Most of my family of origin lives in Illinois, with the exception of one sister now living in Michigan. I consider my husband's family as part of my family, since I met my husband when I was 16. In order to be able to keep in touch with our families, we need to have their contact information. Now that I am retired and not actively showing up for work each day, I have time! Since we live in Sparks, NV, and have not lived in Illinois since 1972, we really have not gotten to spend a lot of time with our families of origin. I wanted to renew my relationships, especially with all my brothers and sisters. Between my family and my husband's family and their children and grandchildren, there is a lot of family!

In nutshell, I have seven brothers and five sisters and my husband has four brothers and a sister. I have more nieces and nephews and great-nieces and great-nephews than I can count.

Goal - long range:

- Reconnect with my family of origin

Objective(s) - future condition(s):

- Increase the number of conversations held with my brothers and sisters each month

Performance Indicator(s) - current condition(s):

- Number of birthday and anniversary cards sent to family members per month

Do

I decided that the first thing that I needed to do was to get all their contact information. I sent a letter off to each brother and sister from both sides of our family. I asked them to give me their contact information and the contact information for their children and grandchildren.

I put all the information into a Microsoft Excel 2003 spreadsheet and generated lists of addresses, birthdays, and anniversaries. I made this my Christmas present to my family and this was no simple task. There are 115 lines on the Microsoft Excel 2003 spreadsheet. My goal for the year is to send each one of them a plain old fun birthday card. I purchased a simple fun birthday card and envelop for $.44. I hope if I am lucky, within time, they will reciprocate and send me a fun card on my birthday and I can go into my later years with lots of well wishes on my birthdays. I just wonder how many of them will get a kick out of getting a birthday card from their aunt, and for some, their great-aunt. This is time well spent!

Check

In the letter I sent out, I asked each of them to check their family contact information. I figured I probably made some input mistakes. I was right! The family spent time at the family Christmas party laughing about the errors in the ages on the birthday list. One sister, who will be 60 this year, was glad to see she would be the same age as one of our younger brothers due to one of my typing errors. Therefore, after checking the other birthdays for accuracy, I sent the list out to everyone who had an e-mail address.

Review

Once a year, I have committed to reviewing the list, adding the names of those who have been born (and in my family that happens almost every year), changing e-mail and physical addresses of those who have moved. As one retires from the everyday work world, they soon learn they have a lot of time on their hands. One must remember that others in their life who are not retired may not yet have as much time to share.

> **Time Management Outcome – Find Your Time by Creating Contacts for the Family**
>
> Because you have taken care of other dimensions in your life you now have time you need to renew relationships with you family of origin. You may want to share more of your time with your family of origin. You may want to focus on what is going on in their lives. For me, the need to renew relationships with my family of origin is paying off. Even as I write this book – my nephew just called to thank me for sending him a birthday card. A 40-year-old man found happiness in getting a "little birthday card" amongst all the other junk and bills. In addition, his call made my day!

Preparing Agendas When Dealing with Professionals

We all have many different relationships with the professionals that help us navigate through modern society, including physicians, attorneys, and investment counselors. We interact with professionals in meetings generally at their offices. Meetings, more meetings, and more meetings consume your time. It is interesting to look up the definition of meeting on Wikipedia. According to Wikipedia, a meeting occurs when "two or more people come together for the purpose of discussing a (usually) predetermined topic such as business or community event planning, often in a formal setting."[40] While this definition focuses on business or community event planning, meetings occur informally throughout your day as you meet with a variety of individuals.

Assess

- Do you plan for the meetings you have in and outside your work environment?
- Do you write an agenda?
- Do you assign time limits to each agenda item?
- Do you ask the one you are meeting with how much time they have to meet with you when you start the meeting?
- Do you keep focused on the agenda items?
- Do you review the tasks that you and the other person(s) need to do before you meet again?
- Do you plan your next meeting before you finish your current meeting?
- Do you keep minutes of your meetings?

Plan

You may be yawning at this point, just thinking this is too much trouble and that it will take time and planning. Yes, it will take time, but working on the process of setting up the environment for a good meeting helps ensure a good outcome for the time spent. An agenda is simply a list of those things you desire to talk about at the meeting. It is wise to ask the people you are meeting with if they have any items they would like to discuss and add them to the agenda. Thinking about what it is you want to talk about before you are in the meeting helps you clear your mind. Be sure to place the priority items early on the agenda.

Goal - long range:

- Prepare agendas when meeting with professionals

Objective(s) - future condition(s):

- To determine if there are any professionals I will be meeting with in the near future and prepare an agenda in advance for the meeting monthly

Performance Indicator(s) - current condition(s):

- Number of scheduled appointments with professionals completed with agenda

Do

See Figure 9 below for an example agenda that I prepared prior to meeting with my investment counselor. The topics will change based on the financial interests you have and your goals and objectives.

Meeting with Investment Counselor
Agenda
January 12, 2009
10:00 – 10:45

- Who bought investment firm? – 5 minutes
- Review of stock market – Investment Counselor's thoughts – 10 minutes
- Review of portfolio – 10 minutes
- How is Roth IRA performing with retirement funds from hospital? – 5 minutes
- Mortgage, next steps? – 5 minutes
- Paperwork from investment firm has decreased, thanks – 1 minute
- Any other issues, ideas, or concerns? – 8 minutes
- When should we meet again? – 1 minute

Figure 9. Agenda for Meeting with Investment Counselor

Check

Take time to do a little analysis when you get home. While you may not do formal minutes for this type of encounter, it is important to make notes to yourself, specifically noting what you need to do before you meet again. Also, note any second thoughts or unanswered questions that you have. It is important, of course, to do the tasks you agreed to do with the investment counselor and to start to build the agenda for the next meeting.

Review

Your meetings with your investment counselor will occur as frequently as you both determine the need to meet. The important thing is to remember to go with an agenda, to be on time, and to get in and out of the office. Each time you meet with the professional, you will appear organized. It is important that you know what it is you need to talk about, what your questions are, and that you are ready to engage in the process. When you go to the meetings with a prepared agenda, you come across as an organized person who wants to accomplish things, not just chat. When you hand the person you are meeting with a single sheet with the word agenda at the top and a few bullet points, you are indicating you are there to do business. Try looking at the time you spend with your doctor as a meeting, prepare an agenda, and the result should reflect more outcomes that are productive.

Time Management Outcome – Finding Your Time by Preparing Agendas When Dealing with Professionals

You should view any meeting with a professional as seriously as any meeting that you might have within your work environment. The younger you are when you start the process of meeting regularly with professionals and going prepared with an agenda and the tasks completed from your last meeting, the earlier you will gain confidence in managing your life situations, saving you a lot of time.

Sandie Barrie

Cherishing Options When Making Friends

Life seems to be spinning around with so many things to do to keep all the necessary things of modern life going. We have to bring in money. We have to buy goods. We have to prepare meals, take care of our minds and bodies, and pay all the bills. We may or may not want to interact with our family. While we do not choose our family, we do choose our friends.

My husband and I, like so many other people, are busy with our work and family environments. Over the years, we have been lucky to have another couple in our lives who have been our friends for nearly 35 years. We have shared the good times and the bad times – the day when the helicopter flew their son to the hospital, the day my husband tried to teach our male friend how to fly over the direction line, and the fun motorcycle rides going down winding roads. My husband and I each have our separate friends, too, and we take time to meet and make new friends. My latest new friend is a sewing buddy whom I enjoy going out to lunch with and sharing our lives and our sewing ventures.

To have a friend, though, you have to be a friend. This means that you have to take the time to see how they are doing and to determine how you want to spend time together. How much time we spend with our friends differs for each one of us – I have some friends that I only talk with a couple times a year, but each time, the conversation starts up with where we left off without missing a beat. Other friends I see every week and truly miss them if they do not call or I do not call to see how they are doing. Then there is my life mate, who, if I didn't hear from him every few hours, I would definitely think something was wrong.

Assess

- How many friends do you have?
- What do you do to make sure your friends want to continue being your friends?
- Are you opening yourself up to make new friends?

Plan

The last question really hit home for me, I wanted some new friends. As I have gotten into my retirement and away from the day-to-day job situation, I am beginning to realize how important it is for me to have contact with others. I want relationships with people. I have started to give a lot of thought to how and what kind of relationships I want for the rest of my life. So here, I am at age 63, trying to figure out how to make some new friends. Not sure that I was going to find a book on this topic, I went to http://www.amazon.com and looked anyway. To my amazement, I found a great book to help me on my journey. The title of the book is, *The Friendship Crisis: Finding, Making, and Keeping Friends When You Are Not a Kid Anymore* by Marla Paul. One concept Paul describes is how to make a community of friends.

Goal - long range:

- Determine strategies to make new friends and to maintain old friends

Objective(s) - future condition(s):

- To identify how to make a community of friends
- To determine the type of community of friends that will give energy to my life
- To start the work towards making a community of friends

Performance Indicator(s) - current condition(s):

- Number of new contacts per month for desired community

Do

The number of people I meet has shrunk significantly over the last year since I retired. So in order for me to develop some new friendships, I have to take some risks and find activities that interest me that I want to be involved in and actually venture out to increase the number of contacts I have related to this new community. To do this, I will have to step outside of my comfort zone and try to determine where I am going to find people who are in similar situations, with time on their hands to develop new relationships. Much to my surprise, I found a great website for meeting up with people face-to-face in my local environment at http://www.meetup.com/ . On this website, you can type in your ZIP code and then find local groups of people who are meeting on special interests, such as sewing, being an entrepreneur, or riding motorcycles.

Check

After I have made new contacts, it will be important for me to treat them like my old, cherished friends. I will need to extend invitations to spend time with these people and hope that they extend invitations to me, as well. It is important to realize that you must check on your friends. When was the last time you called your friends, sent them an e-mail, or went to their Facebook page? Relationships grow over time with contact. My husband and I routinely have dinner with our old cherished friends. We look forward to the time we spend with our friends. We make sure that we do not overextend our welcome with those that we choose to share our lives.

Review

Sometimes, and for a variety of reasons, we may grow apart from our friends or we may decide that nourishing the relationship is no longer of value to us or to the other person. Other times, a new friend may bring some vitality into our lives, allowing us to see new and different perspectives. As we age, we will need to continue learning how to make friends with those individuals that bring energy to our lives.

Find Your Time: Assess, Plan, Do, Check, Review

> **Time Management Outcome – Find Your Time by Cherishing Options When Making Friends**
>
> If anywhere in your life you have options, you have options when you choose your friends. You need to cherish those people you call your friends.
>
> If you are holding on to a relationship that is not bringing health and happiness to your life, let it go. Wasting time on relationships that you have outgrown takes time away from developing new, refreshing relationships. However, most of all, if you are like my husband and I, when you are lucky enough to find relationships that you enjoy, cherish the option and keep on working on maintaining your common interests. Remember, there is no joy like finding a new friend – it adds spark to your life and brings joy and happiness to your existence.

In summary, see Appendix A for suggested performance indicators for building relationships. While you can use Microsoft Word 2003 or Microsoft Excel 2003 to develop this form, paper and pencil will accomplish the same goal of recording information on a monthly basis. Appendix B provides additional situations for the building relationships dimension where you can explore using the quality improvement model to make changes you desire in your life. The Selected Resources Section provides reference materials to help you as you develop your plan. Now that we have evaluated and put in place better systems for our building relationships dimension, we can turn to managing change with others.

What is Coming Up?

At the beginning of Section 5, I explained how a pilot needed both vertical and horizontal control to keep the plane flying and to avoid a crash. The focus of Section 5 revolved around the 10 life dimensions from a vertical perspective using 30 relevant situations. In each situation, a short vignette set the stage to ask you to examine how you could find your time using the quality improvement model. As I mentioned, the vertical control has the pilot focusing on the airplane itself and whether there is enough gas, the radios are working, and the instructions from the tower are coming across loud and clear. Once the pilot leaves the runway, he needs to focus his attention horizontally to include the changing weather and the other planes that are in the same airspace. Next, in Section 6, we will focus our attention on the horizontal perspective as we explore how to merge our life dimensions and the changes you are working on within each life dimension with the changes in life dimensions that are occurring with those whom you live: family, friends, and co-workers.

Section 6 – Blending Your Change with the Change of Others

When it is all said and done, we do control a lot of what goes on in your life, but there is also a lot that goes on that we do not control, can not control, or do not want to control. When looking at the vertical control perspective for 30 situations the focus was on the situation itself as if there were nothing else going on in our life. The quality improvement model provided a system to examine the situation in order to make improvements. Now, in Section 6, we will examine the horizontal control perspective, which is, how we go about managing all of your life dimensions and the changes you are making in your life – and coordinating your changes with the changes others are making in their lives. How you go about living your life, coping with the inevitable changes and choices that are a part of life, has a lot to do with your perspectives and personality or what we call, "style."

Authors Sunny Schlenger and Roberta Roesch explain in their book, *How to be Organized in Spite of Yourself,* that one's organizational ability is greatly dependent on their personal style. Schlenger and Roesch describe 10 different personal styles and offer suggestions on how to handle time and space issues. While the material presented by Schlenger and Roesch is an interesting read, many of us do not want to take the time to do the self-analysis to determine what our organizational style is, nor do we want to go through the necessary work to identify the strategies that will inherently work with that organizational style.

After reviewing many authors, I am offering a few ideas that work well with the quality improvement model presented in *Find Your Time: Assess, Plan, Do, Check, Review.* What follows are suggestions to assist you in being able to move forward with the changes you desire in your life as you interact with those you work with and live with, and even those you pass by in the stores.

Daily and Weekly Review

Perhaps one of the most important things you can do to be successful in making a change is to keep the desired change in front of you by reviewing what it is that you want daily and weekly. This does not need to take much of your time, just review the short time management templates that you developed for the situations of the life dimension(s) that you want to change (see Section 7 below). Using the time management template will help you keep focused on what you desire, how you plan to do it, and the actions you need to take. It is amazing how, even when the activities only allow you to take one or two small steps in a day toward the change, that the steps taken lead to the desired outcome. It is important to share with your family and friends what you need to do. If you find interruptions in your day, you can play a game with yourself, after you have done something someone else wants you to do, do one thing that you want to do.

Learn Tools

Technological and non-technological tools were showcased in Section 4 to assist in managing your time. Selecting one of these tools and making use of it in your daily life will contribute to better management of your time. There is a learning curve associated with any new technological tool you choose, and adding specific time to learn about the new tool to your calendar will help you in managing your time as you work through what it is you want to change. It is necessary to realize that the other people you interact with may not want to use any technological tools or may want to use different ones than you use.

Nurture Relationships

As you move through life, there will be difficulties, times where you feel in control of your life and environment, and times when you do not feel in control of anything. Having someone you can call at the last minute who will run and get your kids from school, jump into the Bunco game in an hour, or someone you can call when your son is being helicoptered to the local hospital post-motorcycle accident are extremely important.

There are also times when our friends will call on us when we are tired, lonely, or just don't want to go out into the snow one more time. What we know is that having an attitude of genuinely wanting to help others has a way of reciprocating when our day needs a little help. What goes around comes around. Maintaining relationships takes precious time, but the time is well spent!

Perception is Everything

Remember that perception is what someone else thinks about you, about your changes, about what it is you are trying to do with your life. Each day take a few minutes and examine how you are coming across to other people. Evaluate if your approach is working for you in reaching your goals and objectives. Understand that it is okay to change your perspective if you learn something new.

Keep Priorities Straight

Most books written about time management discuss priorities. One model that Allen describes in *Getting Things Done: The Art of Stress-Free Productivity* is the "threefold model for evaluating daily work."[43] The three models include: doing predefined work, doing work as it shows up, or defining your work. While most of us would like to do things, we want to work on or work that we have previously predefined; many of us end up doing work as it shows up.

How you handle the work that shows up – as surprises or interruptions – will reflect on your capacity to be successful in your efforts to make the changes you want in your life. Once you understand what you want to do and become passionate about doing it, natural energy will take over and propel you forward. You will be better able to take care of the surprises that come along and then to move on with doing what it is that you have defined in your time management model templates. The more you value your decisions made while developing the templates, the more your self-determination and self-esteem increases.

Maintain Open Options

Perhaps the one gift we can give ourselves in working with others is learning how to maintain a mindset that keeps our options open. As you move through the components of the quality improvement model and learn lessons where you are successful, where you were not quite as successful, or where you may perceive that you right out failed, knowing that there are always options helps maintain your ability to move forward. Moreover, while you know you need to keep your priorities straight, you also must keep your options open. For instance, I never view a call from one of my children or my grandchildren as an interruption. However, if they happen to call just when I have sat down to eat a meal with an old friend, they may have to be told that I can not talk with them right at that moment. I need to understand that keeping my options open allows me the latitude to let them know I cannot talk right at that second unless of course it is an emergency, but that I will call them back later. Then I keep my word.

Understand Your Values

How you make choices is critical to how you spend your time. Your family, friends, school, and work experiences influence your value system. Knowing what you value in life will help you spend your time wisely. Resilience helps you come back repeatedly to your core values as you interact with others.

Balance Persistence and Patience

Knowing that you have decided to make a change in one of the situations in one of your life dimensions is very important. In order for most change to occur, you will have to be persistent in doing what needs to occur. On the other hand, things will happen to prevent you from obtaining your goals even with the best laid out plan, so know that a healthy dose of patience is also needed. Learn resilience early in life because learning how to be tolerant of decisions that do not favor your position bolsters the ability to be persistent and patient with your goals and objectives.

Be Considerate

Every day, we encounter other people in your space. Holding a door for someone else seems so simple and yet the gesture puts a spring in my walk when it happens to me. Saying "thank you" when someone helps you is a small gesture, but it validates whatever was done for you was important to you. How about not being the first person out of the parking lot after church? Do you stand real close to the next person in the grocery line? Consideration for another person who is sharing the same space as you are is important and demonstrates respect.

Setting Your Own Pace

I walked into the truck stop and was quickly overwhelmed with all the people who were moving at different speeds. One man almost walked over me as he darted to the back of the store, looking for something so he could get back to his big rig and back on the road. Have you ever been in line purchasing something with the person behind you seeming to "rush" you by standing too close or starting to talk to the cashier before you make your purchase? Have you ever felt like a product moving down a conveyor belt through the store of life? Pay attention the next time you get in your car after church services and see the strategies different people use to move out of the parking lot. Do you fit in to the flow of traffic as you determine the best line to purchase your food in the grocery store? What do you do if you forget something? How does your driving speed compare to the other drivers on your morning commute?

We all move at different paces. Some people are small and some are large. Some people are old with disabilities. Some people are young and athletic. While you can't stop people from moving faster or slower than you do, you can respect the pace you move at and know that sometimes you have to move faster or slower to match up with the needs of others. However, there are times when you just need to hold your own and respect that you do not always have to adjust to the speed of those in your environment.

Keep in the Present

Much of this book talks about planning for the future or looking at data of what has occurred in the past, but the real power in time management is keeping in the present. If you're driving, then drive; if you are planning, then plan; if you are spending time with your children or grandchildren, then spend time with your children or grandchildren. When you take the time to focus on what it is you are doing, you not only have a better chance of doing it right, you have a better chance of enjoying your life and that is what time management is really about. Furthermore, there is less chance for errors or mistakes to occur if you are concentrating on what you are doing. In addition, making fewer errors saves time by not having to redo something.

Smile

Lastly, there is nothing like a genuine happy smile. Share your smiles more and it will save you time as people will be more eager to help you find something in a store. Share your smile and find the dealer willing to listen to you when you are explaining why the car just stops working. A smile makes a good icebreaker when you walk into a strange group of people who are going to make a decision about something important in your life. In other words, you can save time if you have a smile on your face that reflects your inner generosity and desire to walk through the world wanting to give more than you take!

What is Coming Up?

Section 6 provided thoughts on how the changes you desire have to be blended with the reality of change that others in your life may be working on; or with those who may resist the change you desire; or even those who believe that the change they are trying to make in their lives takes priority over the changes that you are trying to make in your life. In Section 7, you can move from reading about change theory and the quality improvement model to using the concepts presented in this book. The Time Management Model template provides a method to assist in working on a situation that is of specific interest to you in one of your life's 10 dimensions. Use the template freely in any work that you are doing. A PDF of the template is located at http://www.findyourtime.org.

Find Your Time: Assess, Plan, Do, Check, Review

Section 7 – Time Management Template

Make a copy of the Time Management Template and get started with one of the desired changes that you identified as you read this book. A copy of this template is located at http://www.findyourtime.org .

Part I - Change Theory

1. What is the **problem** or opportunity you are trying to solve or improve?

2. What **stage** of change are you in?

Part II – Time Management

1. How much **time** are you willing to spend to solve this problem or improve this opportunity?

2. What are you willing to give up to create the **time** needed to solve this problem or improve this opportunity?

Part III - Quality Improvement Model

1. What do you need to **assess** to solve the problem or improve the opportunity?

Sandie Barrie

2. What do you need to find out in order to **develop a plan** to solve the problem or improve the opportunity? Be sure to include goal(s), objective(s) and performance indicator(s).

3. Based on your plan, what do you need to **do** to solve the problem or improve the opportunity? Be sure to develop a check sheet that helps you gain the data needed (in real time) and measure the performance indicator(s) as time passes.

4. At a predetermined point in time, **check** to see if you are making progress on solving the problem or improving the opportunity. Take time to analyze and do not be paralyzed by the task.

5. Based on the results of ongoing performance indicators, what **review** do you need to do to ensure that the change is accomplished or sustained? What will you do to work on solving the problem or improving the opportunity? In addition, once solved, what will you do to share the solution with others?

What is Coming Up?

Section 7 has provided a template for working through a problem or situation requiring change or an opportunity for improvement in one or more of the 10 life dimensions. Section 8 provides my last thoughts on writing Find Your Time: Assess, Plan, Do, Check, Review.

Section 8 – Last Thoughts

I have had the privilege of being the oldest of 13 children born in 16 years (no twins) to the same mom and dad. As I tell people who ask, *"I am the oldest and the shortest in the family."* I married a man who taught me how to be practical, and with him, I have three sons, the joy of our lives – especially when the five grandchildren came along.

I worked in health care for a long time, where I had the opportunity to meet hundreds of people who were suffering, needed help, and wanted relief from their pain, anxiety, or suffering. I never realized it until now, but each of these individuals taught me something about life. Sometimes, they were lessons I did not want to learn. I did learn many things from Oprah, whose show I often watched after coming off a shift. I used to say her show brought me *"comic relief"* from the dramatic health care situations that I had just been in, since many of Oprah's shows have topics that bring a smile to one's face. She has a wide, generous laugh that has often brightened my day.

I went to school for more years than I want to add up. It was not always easy to find the time, the energy, and the resources to go. I was not the "smart student" who had all the answers. I struggled in classes to understand the lessons. Nevertheless, what I did have was a curiosity about life, a strong hunger wanting to learn about things I did not know.

Learning about change theory helped me understand why we don't all accept change at the same time and that the curve of acceptance is different for everybody and everything. Helping me understand where I was on the curve helped me understand when I could actually start to solve a problem or embrace a new skill that interested me. Using the quality improvement model helped me put my goals and objectives in perspective and assisted me in actually obtaining the outcome that I was looking for in my life.

I could not have written *Find Your Time: Assess, Plan, Do, Check, Review* had I not had the experiences I have had with, family, marriage/children, work, and school. I hope you will take some of the suggestions offered and use the concepts of change theory and the quality

Sandie Barrie

improvement model presented here to help you gain more time, energy, and happiness in your life.

I would appreciate if you would take a few minutes to take a short survey about this book on http://www.findyourtime.org. It will help me improve the work that I am doing. Thank you for taking the time to read this book! As I said at the start of the book, I hope that you have enjoyed this venture. Lastly, pass this book onto someone else who needs to find their time.

I didn't create the saying, and I searched Google, but could not figure out who came up with it. Therefore, here are my last words for this book, *"Remember – prior planning prevents poor performance"* and while you are planning, *"take time to stop and smell the roses"*.

Find Your Time: Assess, Plan, Do, Check, Review

Appendix A – Performance Indicators Dashboard by Month

You can keep your check sheet in your call-up file. Once a month, enter the data from you check sheet to your performance indicators dashboard. A simple table provides a method to keep track of the important performance indicators by month. You can develop the table on paper or in Microsoft Word 2003 or Microsoft Excel 2003, (see Table 14 below). Placing the document in your weekly call-up file, say on Mondays, gives you an opportunity to place a mark on an item that you may be counting such as the number of meals eaten in restaurants. Put the Performance Indicators Dashboard by Month form in your call-up file and put a date in your calendar to review your monthly progress. I like the last day of the month.

Table 14 – Sample Performance Indicators by Month for Sandie Barrie 2009

	Jan	Feb	Mar	Apr	May
Current BMI, recorded on last day of month	26.8	26.8	26.8		
Current weight, recorded on last day of month	138	137	136	136	135
Number of painful days for month, recorded on last day of month	2	6	0	10	0
Number of unfiled documents for home medical record, recorded on last day of month	Lots	Lots	Lots	0	0
Copy of updated home medical record placed in safety deposit box, recorded on last day of month	Y	No changes	Y	Y	No changes
Number of meals eaten at home for month, recorded on last day of month	23	22	27	27	27
Number of meals eaten in restaurants for month, recorded on last day of month	8	6	4	3	4
Number of time wasters identified in food preparation and cleanup, recorded on last day of month	0	1	0	1	0
Total number of extra trips to purchase groceries/household items, recorded on last day of month	4	6	3	2	6
Number of times plastic, glass, cans, and discarded computer paper were recycled by month, recorded on last day of month	2	2	2	2	2
Number of hours spent in doing regular	20	22	20	16	26

Sandie Barrie

	Jan	Feb	Mar	Apr	May
laundry by month					
Number of items recorded in My Stuff Deluxe, recorded on last day of month	0	10	30	40	100
Copy of updated My Stuff Deluxe placed in safety deposit box, recorded on last day of month	N	Y	Y	N	Y
Number of times lost when traveling on a short trip per month, recorded on last day of month	5	4	3	3	1
Number of times lost when traveling on a long trip per month, recorded on last day of month	0	2	0	0	0
Maintenance log completed for PT cruiser, recorded on last day of month	Y	Y	Y	Y	Y
Number of dollars in checking account recorded on last day of month, recorded on last day of month	$1000	$1500	$1250	$1383	$1000
Number of dollars in savings account, recorded on last day of month	$2,000	$2100	$2500	$2750	$3000
Number of new credit card expenses, recorded on last day of month	$0	$0	$0	$0	$0
Investment statements reviewed, recorded on last day of month	Y	Y	Y	Y	Y
Journal entry determining comfort level with ability to meet economic needs, recorded on last day of month	Y	Y	Y	Y	Y
Number of volunteer hours, recorded on last day of month	4	4	7	8	6
Resume reviewed and updated, recorded on last day of month	Y	Y	Y	Y	Y
Reviewed whether there are any new educational pursuits desired, recorded on last day of month	Y	Y	Y	Y	Y
Number of classes attended, recorded on last day of month	4	4	4	3	2
Number of requirements/assignments completed by month, recorded on last day of month	0	0	0	0	0
Number of sewing articles completed, recorded on last day of month	3	4	2	1	0
Number of hours playing piano by month, recorded on last day of month	0	0	0	0	0

	Jan	Feb	Mar	Apr	May
Number of books self-published by month, recorded on last day of month	0	0	0	0	0
Number of proposals for volunteer projects written per month, recorded on last day of month	1	0	0	1	0
Number of pounds of food per month donated to church, recorded on last day of month	50	150	200	50	250
Number of glasses donated to nonprofit organizations per month, recorded on last day of month	20	30	20	50	20
Amount of cash for food per month donated to nonprofit organization, recorded on last day of month	$900	$750	$900	$600	$800
Clothes drive held per month, recorded on last day of month	1	0	0	0	0
Number of birthday and anniversary cards sent to family members per month, recorded on last day of month	8	9	10	7	8
Number of scheduled appointments with professionals completed with agendas recorded on last day of month	none scheduled	1	none scheduled	2	1
Number of new contacts made per month, recorded on last day of month	2	3	1	0	1

Appendix B – Examples: Quality Improvement Opportunities

Life Dimensions	Situations for Using the Quality Improvement Model
Health	Preventing falls, insurance processing, improving mental health
Food	Food storage, using coupons to purchase food
Household Maintenance	Cleaning out the garage, shed, or attic; improving landscaping; controlling bugs; storage
Travel	Purchasing a car, selling a car, travel arrangements
Finances	Getting credit; retirement investing and planning; buying and selling real estate
Work	Handling a difficult boss, working with an uncooperative co-worker, mentoring a new graduate
Education	Getting through a boring class, developing a plan for taking classes
Hobbies	Learning about ancestry, getting a pet
Service Opportunities	Collecting baby lay-outs for nurses to dispense at local hospital to moms who cannot afford clothes for newborns; having high school students sell books donated by service group or church on http://www.amazon.com to pay for school band to go to the basketball game; start a neighborhood watch group
Building Relationships	Gaining consensus on family issues, such as selling the inherited piece of land; starting a new club of community interest to you in order to meet new friends

Appendix C – Writing a Proposal Using SOPPADA Format

A SOPPADA allows decision-makers (spouses, bosses, church leaders) to see in a short, no-frills format a specific plan of action. A simple but key factor is presentation, so be sure to leave a lot of white space on the two pages.

Subject	*Put in title. (What would you like to do?)*
Objective	*What do you want to accomplish? Break down into measurable units that you will use to demonstrate the outcome to your colleagues.*
Present Situation	*This will be longer – concisely and realistically, capture the essence of what has gone on in the past and what is going on now.*
Proposal	*This is where you get to say what you want to do. Again, try to be concise and somewhat broad in your description. (Most decision-makers don't need to know how many paperclips they will need to buy).*
Advantages	*Write three **strong** statements of why this is needed.* • • •
Disadvantages	*Write three statements of what the disadvantages might be and be careful not to ruin your case by overstating the disadvantages.* • • •
Action	*Write action-oriented statements; be proactive and respectful.*
Approval Signature and Date	

Selected Resources

There is a variety of resources available both in print and on the web. I provide my suggestions for further reading on topics discussed in this book. My choices are based on simplicity of presentation and ones that enhance and provide more detail on the materials included in *Find Your Time: Assess, Plan, Do, Check, Review*.

Print Resources by Section

SECTION 1 – INTRODUCTION

In 1998, Randy Pausch gave a lecture to doctoral students and faculty about time management. His short book has useful information about how to handle people and projects that waste your time:

Pausch, R. (2008). Time management. Beta Nu Publishing: Kankakee, IL.

Are you looking for a list of tips on how to save time? Check out these two resources:

Leland, K. & Bailey, K. (2008). Time management in an instant: 60 ways to make the most of your day. Career Press: Franklin Lakes, NJ.

Smallin, D. (2004). The one-minute organizer plain & simple. Storey Publishing: North Adams, MA.

St. James, E. (2001). Simplify your life: 100 ways to slow down and enjoy the things that really matter. Fine Communications: NY.

Do you have many distractions in your life that make it nearly impossible to spend time learning how to manage your time? Learn more about how to handle your innate procrastination:

Tracy, B. (2006). Eat that frog! 21 great ways to stop procrastination and get more done in less time. Berrett-Koehler Publishers, Inc.: San Francisco, CA.

SECTION 2 – CHANGE THEORY

Learn from the gurus of diffusion of innovations and change theory:

Rogers, E. (2003). Diffusion of innovations. 4th Ed. The Free Press: NY.

Prochaska, J.O., Norcoss, J., DiClemente, C. (1994), <u>Changing for good: A Revolutionary six-stage program for overcoming bad habits and moving your life positively forward</u>. Avon Books, Inc.: NY.

Want to see how the thinking on change management has evolved?

Cameron, E. & M. Green (2009). <u>Making sense of change management: A complete guide to the models, tools & techniques of organizational change, 2nd Ed</u>. Kogan Page Limited: USA.

SECTION 3 – QUALITY IMPROVEMENT MODEL

If you want to read the early works on statistical control charts, which underlies the work on performance indicators, see:

Shewhart, W. A. (1986). <u>Statistical method from the viewpoint of quality control</u>. Dover Publications: NY.

The leader of the quality management movement is Edward Deming, who was a sophisticated thinker, and whose writings are somewhat difficult to understand, but if you are growing passionate about the quality improvement topic, you will want to read:

Deming, W. E. (2000). <u>Out of the crisis</u>. Massachusetts Institute of Technology: Cambridge, MA.

Need how to learn how to write goals and objectives? This resource is very helpful:

Roulillard, L.A. (2003). <u>Goals and goal setting: Achieving measured objectives (3rd Ed.)</u>. Crisp Publications, Inc.: USA.

SECTION 4 – TOOLS

Never used the Internet or are a novice and want to learn how to use the Web effectively? Do you want a quick, fun way to learn? If so, run out and get this book today:

Krug, S. (2006). <u>Don't make me think! A common sense approach to web usability, 2nd Ed</u>. New Riders: Berkeley, CA.

Heard the word "BlackBerry" one time too many times and want to determine exactly what this is and how it can help you? Check out:

Kao, R. & Sarigumba, D. (2009). BlackBerry for dummies. Wiley Publishing, Inc.: Hoboken, NJ.

Learn from a best-selling author on how to set up your productivity system that does not focus on technological tools to manage stuff that comes into your life:

Allen, D (2001). Getting things done: The art of stress-free productivity. Penguin Group: NY.

Want to learn what to consider when purchasing a paper or electronic planner and how to map out your time in your planner? Check out:

Morgenstern, J. (2004). Time management: From the inside out. Owl Books: NY.

Want to review the most common time management ideas? Check out:

Dodd, P., and Sundheim, D. (2009). The 25 best time management tools & techniques: How to get more done without driving yourself crazy. Peak Performance Press: Chelsea, MI.

Learn more tips on how to use Microsoft Outlook to manage your time:

McGhee, S. (2005). Take back your life! Microsoft Press: Redmond, WA.

If you want to learn about the breadth of social media and apply it to your business life, then don't miss this book:

Evans, D. (2008). Social media marketing: An hour a day. Wiley Publishing: Indianapolis, IN.

SECTION 5 - DIMENSIONS OF LIFE

Health

Are you interested in learning more about how our bodies work, how we age, and what we can do to slow down the aging process?

Roizen, M. F. & Oz, M. C. (2008). You: The owner's manual, updated and expanded edition: An insider's guide to the body that will make you healthier and younger. Harper Collins Publisher: NY.

Have you become a patient and specifically want to understand how you can navigate the health care delivery system?

Sandie Barrie

Roizen, M. F. & Oz, M.C. (2006). You: The smart patient: an insider's handbook for getting the best treatment. Free Press: NY.

Food

So you want to save some time on food preparation…check out:

Fox, L., Ed. (2005). Betty Crocker's cookbook: Everything you need to know to cook today, 10th Ed. Wiley Publishing: NY.

…And save money while you are doing it? Then be sure to read this popular book by the Economides:

Economides, S. & Economides, A. (2007). America's cheapest family gets your right on the money: Your guide to living better, spending less, and cashing in on your dreams. Random House Inc.: NY.

Household Maintenance

A great book filled with lots of suggestions on how to organize your home: Wilska, Emily. (2009). Organizing your home. Morris Publishing: Guilford, CT.

Recently shown on Oprah's show, see:

Walsh, P. (2007). It's all too much: An easy plan for living a richer life with less stuff. Simon & Schuster, NY.

Have too much stuff and need help storing your possessions? See:

Smallin, D. (2009). The one-minute storage solutions: A to Z storage solutions. Storey Publishing: North Adams, MA.

Need a practical guide on doing laundry? Check out:

Mendelson, C. (2005). Laundry: The home comforts book of caring for clothes and linens. Scribner: NY.

Finances

Consistency is the message in managing your finances (credit, retirement investment, savings, spending, real estate and paying for college) in these challenging times as reflected in Suze Orman's 2009 book:

Orman, Suze (2008). Suze Orman's 2009 action plan: Keeping your money safe and sound. Spiegel & Grau: NY.

Travel

Do you have travel plans in your future? Then you can't miss this exciting book:

Stellin, S. (2006). How to travel practically anywhere: The ultimate planning guide. Houghton Mifflin Company: NY.

Work

Want to learn more about your personality and what work might be right for you? Check out:

Tieger, P.D. and Barron-Tieger, B. (2007). Do what you are: Discover the perfect career for you through the secrets of personality type – Revised and Updated Edition. Little, Brown & Company: London.

Trying to change careers? See a book that has helped me several times with over 30 years in publication and renewed each year:

Bolles, R.N. (2009). What color is your parachute? 2009: A practical manual for job-hunters and career-changers. Ten Speed Press: Berkeley, CA.

If you are retired, been off for a few months or a year and wonder just what you are going to do with the rest of your time, check out:

Bolles, R. N. & Nelson, J. E. (2007) What color is your parachute? For retirement planning now for the life you want. Ten Speed Press: Berkeley, CA.

If you are going for a specific job, this book is filled with tips to help you snag the interview and get the job:

Shapiro, C. (2008). What does somebody have to do to get a job around here? 44 insider secrets that will get you hired. St. Martin's Press: NY.

So you have never written a resume, wrote your last resume over 10 years ago, or just want to know what to include and not include? Then this book and CD are for you:

Mayer, D. (2008). How to write & design a professional resume to get the job: Insider secrets you need to know – With companion CD-ROM. Atlantic Publishing Group, Inc.: Ocala, Florida.

Sandie Barrie

<u>Education</u>

Are you looking for a candid book on whether a college education is going to get you what you need or want? Check out:

Norhanian, A. (2009). <u>College is for suckers: The first college guide you should read</u>. iUniverse: Bloomington, ID.

<u>Hobbies</u>

See http://www.amazon.com **for information on hundreds of hobbies. Specifically for sewing, learning to play the piano, and writing, see my favorite choices:**

<u>Sewing</u>
Are you trying to learn how to sew? Then this basic book, written by a seamstress who has been teaching for many years, will serve you well.

<u>Colgrove, D. (2008). Sewing visual quick tips</u>. Wiley Publishing: NJ.

<u>Music</u>
I can't really rave about these two books yet, as far as being successful in learning how to play the piano, but I have reviewed them and they are written simply. Check out and see what you think.

Cooper, H. (2007). <u>How to read music in 3 easy lessons</u>. Metro Books: NY.

Freeth, N. (2007). <u>Learn to play the piano and keyboard: A step-by-step guide</u>. Parragon: UK.

<u>Writing</u>
Here is an experienced author on the topic of writing books. I have been following his work for years and have found he provides helpful information.

Poynter, D. (2009). <u>Dan Poynter's self-publishing manual, Volume 2: How to write, print and sell your own book</u>. Para Publishing: Santa Barbara, CA.

Service Opportunities

Perhaps one of the most generous people in contemporary society was Randy Pausch, who gave of himself. His book places a realistic perspective on our use of time and how we can enable the dreams of others. If you are looking for inspiration to do more service opportunities, you don't want to miss the opportunity to read:

Pausch, R. (2008). The last lecture. Hyperion: NY.

While there are many books on volunteerism and volunteer efforts, I recently had the privilege of hearing Scott Miller discuss how to end poverty by developing a circle around a family in poverty and working with them through members of the community to take on changing the issues. If you would like to work in this area, do take time to read:

Miller, S. (2007). Until it's gone: Ending poverty in our nation in our lifetime. aha! Process, Inc.: Highlands, TX

Relationships

If you want to learn how to say something when you are talking, then this book is for you.

Lowndes, L. (2003). How to talk to anyone: 92 little tricks for big success in relationships. McGraw Hill: NJ.

If you need some sage advice on developing friendships, don't miss the opportunity to read this engaging book:

Paul, M. (2004). The friendship crisis: Finding, making, and keeping friends when you are not a kid anymore. Rodale: PA.

In addition, if you are having problems with your primary relationship reading Dr. Phil's book may give you some new ideas:

McGraw, P. (2000). Relationship rescue: A seven-step strategy for re-connecting with your partner. Hyperion: NY.

Sandie Barrie

SECTION 7 – BLENDING CHANGE WITH OTHERS

Do you desire to know more about your organizational style? Then see:

Schlenger, S. and Roesch, R. (1999). How to be organized in spite of yourself. Penguin Group: NY.

Websites by Section

Section 1 - Introduction
Amazon Self-publishing website:	http://createspace.com
Find Your Time Website, hosting copies templates from book:	http://www.findyourtime.org
Source for Post-it Highlighter Pen:	http://www.amazon.com

Section 3 – Quality Improvement Model
Calculate Body Mass Index:	http://www.nhlbisupport.com/bmi/bmicalc.htm

Section 4 – Time Management Tools
Save Favorite Search List to the World Wide Web:	http://www.diigo.com/index
Online (peer-edited) encyclopedia:	http://www.wikipedia.org
Find a common definition of a term:	http://www.m-w.com
Social Media Websites for Author:	http://www.facebook.com/SandieBarrie
	http://www.linkedincom/in/SandieBarrie
	http://twitter.com/SandieBarrie
Find directions between to places:	http://www.mapquest.com
Find a location on the earth:	http://earth.goggle.com/
Make a computer-to-computer visual connection:	http://www.skype.com
Website to buy or sell something:	http://www.craigslist.com

Section 5 - Using Time to Manage Life Dimensions
Health
Calculate Body Mass Index:	http://www.nhlbisupport.com/bmi/bmicalc.htm
Calculate Calories:	http://www.caloriecontrol.org/calcalcs.html
Pain Information:	http://www.webmd.com/pain-management/guide/pain-management-overview-facts

Find Your Time: Assess, Plan, Do, Check, Review

Privacy Information: http://www.hhs.gov/ocr/privacy/hipaa/understanding/consumers/index.html

Health Journal: http://utility2.realage.com/media/pdfs/SP_HealthJournal.pdf

Food
Cooking: http://www.bettycrocker.com/store/

Household Maintenance
Software to list belongings: http://www.contactplus.com/products/freestuff/mystuff.htm

Travel
Mapping: http://www.mapquest.com/

Finance
Suze Orman, Finance Guru: http://www.suzeorman.com

Work
Job Hunting: http://www.jobhuntersbible.com
Personality Test: http://www.personalitytype.com/career_quiz

Education
How to Study: http://www.cse.buffalo.edu/~rapaport/howtostudy.html

Hobbies
Beginning Sewing: http://sewing.about.com
YouTube: http://www.youtube.com (Type in any keyword for favorite hobby and see what you find!)

Service Opportunities
1-800-VOLUNTEERS: http://www.1800volunteer.org/1800Vol/openindexaction.do

VolunteerMatch: http://www.volunteermatch.org

Building Relationships
Find a Local Meeting: http://www.meetup.com

Endnotes

[1] Merriam-Webster Online, http://www.merriam-webster.com/dictionary/find, accessed June 17, 2009.

[2] Merriam-Webster, http://www.merriam-webster.com/dictionary/theory, accessed June 17, 2009.

[3] Merriam-Webster, http://www.merriam-webster.com/dictionary/change, accessed June 17, 2009.

[4] Rogers, E. (2003). Diffusion of innovations, 4th Ed. The Free Press: NY, p. 162.

[5] Rogers, E. (2003). Diffusion of innovations, 4th Ed. The Free Press: NY, pp. 263 -266.

[6] Prochaska, J.O., Norcoss, J.C., & DiClemente, C. C. (1994). Changing for good: A revolutionary six-stage program for overcoming bad habits and moving your life positively forward. Avon Books, Inc: NY, pp. 25-35.

[7] Wikipedia, http://en.wikipedia.org/wiki/Wikipedia:About, accessed June 17, 2009.

[8] Wikipedia, http://en.wikipedia.org/wiki/Quality_improvement, accessed April 29, 2009.

[9] Wikipedia, http://en.wikipedia.org/wiki/Model , accessed April 29. 2009.

[10] Deming, E. (2000). Out of the crisis. Massachusetts Institute of Technology: Cambridge, MA.

[11] Wikipedia, http://en.wikipedia.org/wiki/Shewhart, accessed April 30, 2009.

[12] Shewhart, W. A. (1980). Economic control of quality of manufactured product/50th anniversary commemorative issue. American Society for Quality Control: Milwaukee, WI.

[13] Deming, E. (2000). Out of the crisis. Massachusetts Institute of Technology: Cambridge, MA.

[14] Rogers, E. (2003). Diffusion of innovations, 4th Ed. The Free Press: NY.

[15] Prochaska, J.O., Norcoss, J.C., & DiClemente, C. C. (1994). Changing for good: A revolutionary six-stage program for overcoming bad habits and moving your life positively forward. Avon Books, Inc: NY.

[16] Allen, D. (2001). Getting things done: The art of stress-free productivity. Penguin Group: NY, p. 7.

[17] Allen, D. (2001). Getting things done: The art of stress-free productivity. Penguin Group: NY, p. 46.

[18] Morgenstern, J. (2004). Time management: From the inside out. Owl Books: NY, pp. 64 – 66.

[19] Morgenstern, J. (2004). Time management from the inside out 2nd ed. Owl Books: NY, p. 11.

[20] Allen, D. (2001). Getting things done: the art of stress-free productivity. Penguin Group: NY, pp. 20 – 21.

[21] Daschle, T. (2008). Critical: What we can do about the health-care crisis. St. Martin's Press: NY, p. 113.

[22] Fox, L., Ed. (2005). Betty Crocker's cookbook: Everything you need to know to cook today, 10th Ed. Wiley Publishing, Inc.: NY.

[23] Mendelson, C. (2005). Laundry: The home comforts book of caring for clothes and linens. Scribner: NY.

[24] Bach, D. (2002). Smart women finish rich. Broadway Books: New York.

[25] Orman, S. (2008). Suze Orman's 2009 action plan: Keeping your money safe and sound. Doubleday Publishing Group: NY.

[26] Bach, D. (2002). Smart women finish rich. Broadway Books: New York.

[27] Tieger, P. D., & Barbara Barron-Tieger. (2007). Do What You Are: Discover the Perfect Career for You Through the Secrets of Personality Type – Revised and Updated Edition Featuring E-Careers for the 21st Century. Little, Brown & Company: London.

[28] Bolles, D. (2009). What color is your parachute? 2009: A practical manual for job-hunters and career-changers. Ten Speed Press: Berkeley, CA.

[29] Bolles, D. (2009). What color is your parachute? For retirement: Planning now for the life you want. Ten Speed Press: Berkeley, CA.

[30] Wikipedia, http://en.wikipedia.org/wiki/Career, accessed April 30, 2009.

[31] Wikipedia, http://en.wikipedia.org/wiki/Work, accessed April 30, 2009.

[32] Wikipedia, http://en.wikipedia.org/wiki/Job, accessed April 30, 2009.

[33] Britton Whitcomb, S. (2006). Resume magic: Trade secrets of a professional resume writer. 3rd Ed. JIST Works: St. Paul, MN.

[34] Norhanian, A. (2009). College is for suckers: The first college guide you should read. iUniverse: Berkeley, CA.

[35] Rapaport, W. J. (2009). How to study. http://www.cse.buffalo.edu/~rapaport/howtostudy.html , accessed April 29, 2009.

[36] Colgrove, D. (2006). Sewing Visual Quick Tips. Wiley Publishing: NJ.

[37] Cooper, H. (2007). How to read music in 3 easy lessons. Metro Books: NY.

[38] Freeth, N. (2007). Learn to play the piano and keyboard: A step-by-step guide. Parragon: UK.

[39] Evans, D. (2008). Social Media Marketing: An Hour A Day. Wiley Publishing: Indianapolis, ID.

[40] Wikipedia, http://en.wikipedia.org/wiki/Meeting, accessed April 29, 2009.

[41] Paul, M. (2004). The friendship crisis: Finding, making, and keeping friends when you are not a kid anymore. Rodale: PA.

[42] Schlenger, S. and Roesch, R. (1999). How to be organized in spite of yourself. Penguin Group: NY.

[43] Allen, D. Getting things done: The art of stress-free productivity. Penguin Group: NY, p. 50.

Bibliography

Books

Allen, D. (2001). Getting Things Done: The Art of Stress-Free Productivity. Penguin Group: NY.

Bach, D. (2002). Smart Women Finish Rich. Broadway Books: NY.

Bolles, D. (2009). What Color Is Your Parachute? 2009: A Practical Manual for Job-Hunters and Career-Changers. Ten Speed Press: Berkeley, CA.

Bolles, D. (2009). What Color Is Your Parachute? for Retirement: Planning Now for the Life You Want. Ten Speed Press: Berkeley, CA.

Britton Whitcomb, S. (2006). Resume Magic: Trade Secrets of a Professional Resume Writer. 3rd Ed. JIST Works: St. Paul, MN.

Colgrove, D. (2006). Sewing Visual Quick Tips. Wiley Publishing: NJ.

Cooper, H. (2007). How to Read Music in 3 Easy Lessons. Metro Books: NY.

Daschle, T. (2008). Critical: What We Can Do About the Health-Care Crisis. St. Martin's Press: NY

Deming, E. (2000). Out of the Crisis. Massachusetts Institute of Technology: Cambridge, MA.

Evans, D. (2008). Social Media Marketing: An Hour A Day. Wiley Publishing: Indianapolis, ID.

Fox, L., Ed. (2005). Betty Crocker's Cookbook: Everything You Need to Know to Cook Today, 10th Ed. Wiley Publishing: NY.

Freeth, N. (2007). Learn to Play the Piano and Keyboard: A Step-by-Step guide. Parragon: UK.

Mendelson, C. (2005). Laundry: The Home Comforts Book of Caring for Clothes and Linens. Scribner: NY.

Morgenstern, J. (2004). Time Management: From the Inside Out. Owl Books: NY.

Norhanian, A. (2009). College Is For Suckers: The First College Guide You Should Read. iUniverse: Berkeley, CA.

Orman, S. (2008). Suze Orman's 2009 action plan: Keeping your money safe and sound. Doubleday Publishing Group: NY.

Paul, M. (2004). The Friendship Crisis: Finding, Making, and Keeping Friends When You Are Not a Kid Anymore. Rodale: PA.

Prochaska, J.O., Norcoss, J., DiClemente, C. (1994). Changing for Good: A Revolutionary Six-Stage Program for Overcoming Bad Habits and Moving Your Life Positively Forward. Avon Books, Inc.: NY.

Rogers, E. (2003). Diffusion of Innovations, 5th Ed. The Free Press: NY

Schlenger, S. and Roesch, R. (1999). How to be Organized In Spite of Yourself. Penguin Group: NY.

Shewhart, W. A. (1980). Economic Control of Quality of Manufactured Product/50th Anniversary Commemorative Issue. American Society for Quality Control: Milwaukee, WI.

Tieger, P. D., and Barbara Barron-Tieger. (2007). Do What You Are: Discover the Perfect Career for You Through the Secrets of Personality Type – Revised and Updated Edition Featuring E-Careers for the 21st Century. Little, Brown & Company: London.

Websites

Merriam-Webster Online. http://www.merriam-webster.com

Rapaport, W. J. (2009). How to Study. http://www.cse.buffalo.edu/~rapaport/howtostudy.html

Wikipedia. http://www.wikipedia.org

Author Index

Allen, David, 21, 28, 31, 165
Bach, David, *84, 91*
Barron-Tieger, Barbara, *95, 96*
Bolles, Richard, *96, 97, 98, 102*
Britton Whitcomb, Susan, *103*
Colgrove, Debbie, *121*
Cooper, Helen, 126
Daschle, Tom, *41, 42*
Deming, Edward, *11, 13, 15*
Evans, Dave, *131*
Fox, Lori, *52*
Freeth, Nick, *126*
Mendelson, Cheryl, *64*
Morgenstern, Julie, *29, 31*
Norhanian, Apri, *111*
Oprah, *4, 26, 84, 173*
Orman, Suze, *84, 85, 88, 89*
Paul, Marla, *95, 103, 158*
Prochaska, James, *7, 8, 11, 16*
Rapaport, William, *116, 117*
Roesch, Roberta, *163*
Rogers, Everett, *7, 8, 11, 16*
Schlenger, Sunny, *163*
Shewhart, *11, 13, 15*
Shewhart, Walter, *11, 13, 15*
Tieger, Paul, *95, 96*

www.ingramcontent.com/pod-product-compliance
Lightning Source LLC
Chambersburg PA
CBHW080336170426
43194CB00014B/2583